Plant Food

MATTHEW KENNEY · MEREDITH BAIRD · SCOTT WINEGARD

PHOTOGRAPHS BY STACEY CRAMP

GIBBS SMITH
TO ENRICH AND INSPIRE HUMANKIND

First Edition
18 17 16 15 14   5 4 3 2 1

Published by
Gibbs Smith
P.O. Box 667
Layton, Utah 84041

1.800.835.4993 orders
www.gibbs-smith.com

Designed by Rita Sowins/Sowins Design
Printed and bound in Hong Kong

Gibbs Smith books are printed on paper produced from sustainable PEFC-
certified forest/controlled wood source. Learn more at www.pefc.org.
Printed and bound in Hong Kong

Library of Congress Cataloging-in-Publication Data

Kenney, Matthew.
  Plant food / Matthew Kenney, Meredith Baird, Scott Winegard ;
photographs by Stacey Cramp. — First edition.
     pages cm
  Includes index.
  ISBN 978-1-4236-3062-3
  1. Cooking (Vegetables) I. Baird, Meredith. II. Winegard, Scott. III. Title.
  TX801.K45 2014
  641.6'5—dc23
                  2013040212

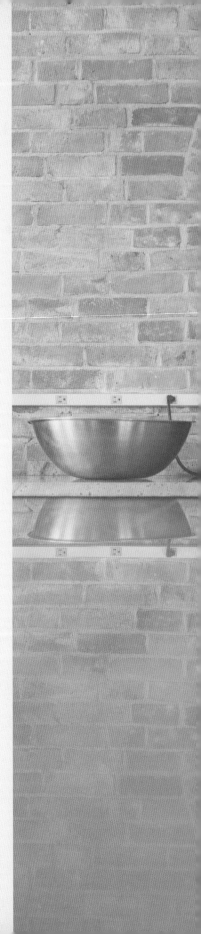

ble o many levels, as a che

Contents

Acknowledgments

Scott and Meredith, for their relentless creativity and brilliant innovation.

Our teams at M.A.K.E. Restaurant, The White Lotus, Tamazul, and The Gothic.

Megan Dunn and her talented instructors.

Our visionary Leadership Team: Don Fields, James Bartolomei, and Juliana Sobral.

Our Strategic Partners, Tamie and David Posnick.

The extraordinary international community who supports us, especially our wonderful students.

Stacey Cramp, for her magic behind the lens.

Michelle Branson and the team at Gibbs Smith.

Rumple.

The new raw food cuisine

MATTHEW

RAW UPDATE

Well here we are 10 years later and still as passionate about raw food as we were on that Monday evening when I had my first reluctant experience with it. Much has changed! Ingredients we had not heard of at that time are readily available, tools and equipment that were never associated with vegetables are now being applied to plant-based cuisine to create incredible flavor, texture, and color, and a global audience now embraces this all as the food of the future. We couldn't be more excited and also proud to be at the forefront of chefs creating food that is both nutritious and delicious.

It was immediately obvious to me that raw food held the potential to change the culinary landscape, from both an artistic and health perspective. Chefs should have a responsibility to prepare foods that not only taste and look good, but also nourish our bodies and carry a deep respect for the environment. Minimally processed fruits, vegetables, nuts, and seeds (plant foods) provide the quickest path to health and also just happen to taste incredible when prepared with the right ingredients, tools, and skills. That's where we come in.

We are constantly innovating and developing new techniques, utilizing modern equipment, and choosing the best ingredients to create dishes that will set a new standard for healthy food. Our work has already been a long and persistent journey, but the discoveries and progress we have made allow us to feel confident that raw, plant-based foods now have a structure supporting them that allows people around the world to prepare them properly, with a well-balanced and delicious approach. We believe that this cuisine is the cuisine of the future and that we are close to a tipping point where all credible chefs and those preparing food will respect the responsibility to nourish those enjoying their meals.

As a company, Matthew Kenney Cuisine's sole mission is to bridge the gap between culinary art and ultimate nutrition. Everything we do is a step toward this goal. As a result, we apply our energies first and foremost into education. In our culinary schools in Santa Monica, California, Miami, Florida, and online, we have trained hundreds of students from over 40 countries to prepare raw foods in a contemporary, artistic manner that embraces the latest

techniques, the best ingredients, and utilizes a structured approach, much like classical French cuisine. This foundation is what will support the growth of the raw food movement in general. Our restaurants serve raw food in settings that resemble any upscale modern dining room, and we cater to clients that range from those utilizing raw food to heal illness to professional athletes interested in enhancing performance. This book is our latest effort to share everything we have learned to allow you to apply those lessons to your own raw foods.

MEREDITH AND SCOTT

Meredith Baird has coordinated the production of our last several books, including our most recent title, *Everyday Raw Detox*, which she wrote entirely on her own. She has a gift for translating our work as chefs to a format which is stylish and yet identifiable to the home cook. Her ability to visualize the end result when pairing a talented photographer, innovative chef, and gorgeous cuisine together is a large part of what makes the style of our books so unique. As a student of fashion, food, and design, she is able to meld these various arts together to deliver a final product that is unique to cookbooks.

I first met Scott Winegard in the kitchen at my first raw food restaurant in New York, in 2004. We were both in the early stages of our raw food journey, although we also recognized that it was something about to be big and this was what brought us to the same place. Over the following years, Scott expanded his culinary experience through travel, experimental dinners, and a stage at the world's number one restaurant, Noma, in Copenhagen. By the time we rejoined, we discovered that our paths were even more aligned than before. We were not only committed to advancing plant-based cuisine, but also to doing it at a level that could compete with any cuisine in the world, not just that made from plants. Scott has applied his unbounded creativity, ingenuity, and talent in such a way that our food has evolved beyond the classics—while we still love raw lasagna from time to time, the new cuisine does not rely as heavily on its cooked or non-plant–based counterparts, and instead stands on its own for what it is. While his personality comes through clearly from the cuisine, I'm also excited to share his insight and quotes throughout the book.

I've been fortunate throughout my career to work with talented chefs, publishers, and photographers. While our food really is as flavorful and beautiful as it appears on the following pages, this is all a result of the team collectively raising the bar.

COMPONENTS OF RAW FOOD

The one question I'm most often asked is simply, "How do you come up with these dishes?" Initially, my ideas were so abstract I had a hard time answering the question. These days, I can comfortably answer, "Based on three factors, elements, technique, and innovation." These also happen to be the areas that define the cuisine of *Plant Food* as well.

ELEMENTS

We hear it all the time these days—the importance of quality ingredients, as well as the benefits of seasonal, local, and organic foods. This could not be more applicable than when speaking of plant-based cuisine. If you shop well, you may rarely go into a supermarket, and instead, if you are fortunate to live in areas that offer local farmers markets, you will find yourself bringing home ingredients that have never seen a refrigerator and may have been harvested just hours before. There is no comparison, and this goes for taste, appearance, and health benefits to sourcing local, fresh ingredients. Not only are your efforts to find the best food rewarded in many ways, shopping is also fun, inspiring for those who like to create, and it gets you outside. Enjoy this process!

TECHNIQUES

In the classes we teach, we devote equal time to technique, including the use of advanced equipment, as we do to creative exercises. When a chef understands how to utilize the latest technology and how to apply technique, they will have far more success in implementing their ideas. In the raw food world there are a number of incredible techniques, and this is why we have selected the chapter titles we used in the book so as to enable you to quickly identify the primary methods we utilize and to highlight the equipment required of these methods. This is not only a unique way to prepare food, but it's also fun, inspiring, and without exception, always emphasizes the retention of nutrients while delivering maximum flavor. While we don't suggest that everyone run out and buy all the latest equipment, we won't deny that these tools are fun to work with and produce remarkable results.

INNOVATION

Once you have identified the freshest and tastiest ingredients and have a solid grasp on the tools of the trade, all that is left to do is to dream. This has always been the part I embraced most—knowledge that you have great ingredients and understand your craft coupled with unbridled imagination is incredibly liberating and just outright enjoyable. Look wherever you are inspired to create your own cuisine—I like to look at fashion, art, and music, although my deepest source of inspiration is nature. Exploring the inherent character of an ingredient always yields the best results.

I remain incredibly thankful for having the opportunity during this place in time to work with such magical food, to have the ability to improve the health of many while respecting the environment, and for being surrounded by art and talent each and every day. One could not ask for more out of a career, and I intend to continue devoting myself to carrying our mission forward.

MEREDITH

Working on our books is probably one of the most fulfilling parts of my job. A book is a work of art. Every word, every photo, every recipe, is strategically selected and created in order to inspire our readers. When you put it out there—it's out—people from all walks of life come to the bookstore, or shop online, and find your creation. The whole concept never ceases to amaze me. My own journey into this career began with a love of books—most specifically, vegetarian cookbooks. From a very young age, I became obsessed with reading vegetable-centric cookbooks. I loved reading the recipes, learning about different ingredients, cultures, flavors, and spices. You can learn so much about life from a cookbook. A cookbook is not just about practical application; it is a medium to become a student of the world. I feel very blessed to have my hand in this industry.

It was seeing Matthew's first raw food cookbook, *Raw Food, Real World* on the center table at Barnes and Noble that I made the leap of faith to attend a raw food culinary school in Northern California. Coming from South Carolina with only a dream and a vision, I had no idea what to expect. At the time, no one seemed to understand that raw food was not only healthy, it was truly a culinary art, and needed to be recognized in that landscape— except, of course, Matthew. Needless to say, my life completely shifted. Doors opened and things started to make sense. I made friends and met kindred spirits. Everything started to "feel right." I suppose this is what it means to follow your passions. It was shortly after my culinary school attendance that I met Matthew in a bit of serendipity. Clearly I was onto something. I followed my own path for a few years, and in 2008, I joined Matthew in a new phase of culinary transformation. Matthew is a true visionary and the amount we have accomplished over this short period of time is amazing.

My role as part of the Matthew Kenney Culinary Team has shifted so much over the years. One of my first tasks for the company was a book—*Everyday Raw Desserts*. Not to put words in his mouth, but I think that Matthew quickly recognized this was a job I was good at. I love the organization, creativity, and delivery of a book. The realization of immediate and permanent results is empowering. Since then I have been an integral part of each of our books on both the recipe development and design. This book has been particularly inspiring for me because I was able to work with the ultra-talented Scott Winegard.

Scott has a certain magic with food. He has taken our cuisine to the next level. You can look at a dish and think that it is unusual, or all about presentation, or not understand it—but when you taste it, you immediately recognize that not only was it arranged to perfection— the flavor was precisely thought out. I am completely sincere in this explanation. I have had more memory sensory experiences with Scott's food than I have ever had in my life. Sometimes, when I taste a dish—I get giddy. The flavor is so incredibly and unexpectedly delicious. Creating beautiful food that tastes good is really quite a challenge. It's an art.

This book embodies the art of culinary art. Whether you take it upon yourself to actually use the recipes, or just savor the visual experience—you won't be disappointed. Every sense is touched. This is a book to read and savor, whether or not you ever take a bite!

SCOTT

I am a little bit obsessed with cookbooks. I collect them, I pour through them all the time, and I anxiously wait for new ones from chefs and restaurants that I follow and that I find inspiration in. There are quite a few in my collection that I own multiple copies of and some that the covers and pages are barely holding on.

I own both of Matthew's books before he focused on raw food, and was drawn to the simple but clean layout with really great photos of beautifully plated dishes. That definitely overflowed into the next 8 books that now focus on our plant-based style.

Matthew and Meredith were talking about the "next book," so I knew there was another cookbook coming. I hoped to be able to help and to see it come together and be a part of that process. When Matthew mentioned that we needed to get started on the next book, I was immediately excited to start. When he approached me with the idea of working on his next book together as collaboration, I said yes, probably before he finished the question.

Matthew has been nothing but supportive and inspiring to me with my approach to raw food. I feel very fortunate to have the guidance and the freedom to create dishes I really enjoy eating.

From the beginning to the end, I thoroughly enjoyed the process, from the recipe writing and testing, to finding photo props, to the plating, to working with Matthew, Meredith, and Stacey. It just got me so excited where the work didn't feel like work and the time just flew by.

Spending most of this year getting to know the farmers at the Santa Monica Farmers Market and having some of the highest quality fruits and vegetables at our reach helped a lot of these recipes come to life. We have no excuse to serve anything but the best quality and that gives us the advantage so we can keep recipes simple and let the natural produce flavors stand on their own. Of course, we coax the produce along with great cold press oils, vinegars, lots of bright fresh herbs, and high quality sea salt and spices. We also get to use some great new and advanced equipment. You don't need it all, but there are some great new techniques that get us some great tasting results.

This opportunity to introduce our modern style really aligns us with our peers in the industry and sets us aside by maintaining a healthy approach to modern cuisine.

ALTHOUGH I ENTERED THE CULINARY WORLD WITH VERY LITTLE COOKING EXPERIENCE, I was fortunate to grow up on the coast of Maine where natural resources are in abundance and seasonality is extremely defined. From as early as I can recall, my family would embrace the bounty of each season, foraging for fiddleheads, tapping maple trees, and appreciating what the earth provided us. As the food industry has gone away from natural over time, and packaged or processed foods are becoming so inexpensive and readily available, it is more important than ever to reconnect with our earth. There is no more natural way of eating. *—MK*

I have always been interested in the idea of eating foods that grow in the wild. It's the most natural and close to nature you can get. Nothing tastes better than fruits and vegetables freshly picked from their branch or vines. Adding the harvest from the natural habitat only enhances that connection between us and our food sources.

Last year I was lucky to be in Oklahoma City during the perfect time for morels. I talked a few instructors and students at Matthew Kenney Oklahoma City into going out and seeing what we could find. The first day we found roughly 10 pounds of morels, plus lots of chickweed and wood sorrel. I'll never forget when we happened upon the first patch of morels— it was probably one of my favorite foraging experiences ever. I still get super excited thinking about that day.

There are definitely some important rules to foraging: Don't touch it if you aren't definitely sure you know what it is, respect the land and only take what you need, and make sure you are far away from pollution as heavy metals store in the roots of many forgeable foods. *—SW*

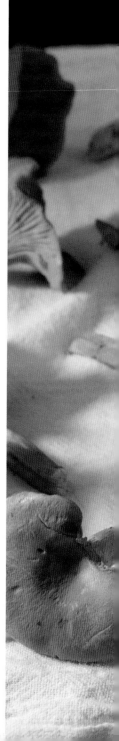

Found

Asparagus and Samphire.
JUNIPER MUSTARD.

I had never thought of mustard as a food until I asked Meredith what her favorite food was one day. "Mustard" was the answer, and since then, I suppose it is a food. Nonetheless, it's phenomenal with earthy, briny dishes such as this. —*MK*

ASPARAGUS AND SAMPHIRE
1 bunch medium asparagus
1 tablespoon lemon juice
1 tablespoon olive oil
Pinch of sea salt
1 cup samphire (sea beans)

JUNIPER MUSTARD
1/2 cup yellow mustard seeds
1/4 cup mustard powder
1/2 cup agave nectar
1/2 cup apple cider vinegar
1/2 cup filtered water
1 tablespoon salt

ASPARAGUS AND SAMPHIRE Trim asparagus all the same length, taking most of the stalk off. Slice asparagus in half vertically. Toss with lemon juice, oil, and salt. Using a vacuum sealer, place in a vacuum bag and seal at 100 percent. This will marinate and compress the dressing into the asparagus.

Pick through samphire and remove stems and beans with dark spots. Rinse with cold water and spin dry with a salad spinner.

JUNIPER MUSTARD Rinse mustard seeds with hot water. Mix mustard powder, agave nectar, vinegar, water, and salt together; add mustard seeds. Store in a sealable glass jar.

ASSEMBLY Remove asparagus from bag and place on top of samphire on individual serving plates. Serve with Juniper Mustard on the side or by tossing like a salad.

Chanterelle Puntarelle.
CUCUMBER DILL.

The word says it all, "chanterelle." It defines elegance, happens to be a beautiful mushroom with a rich golden hue, has the ideal texture, and is just incredible raw as well. —*MK*

CHANTERELLES
1 cup chanterelles, cleaned
1 tablespoon lemon juice
1 tablespoon olive oil
Pinch of sea salt

CUCUMBER
1 cucumber, peeled and
  seeded

$1/4$ cup fresh dill, finely minced
1 teaspoon lemon zest
Sea salt

DILL OIL
2 cups chopped fresh dill,
  including stems
1 cup olive oil
1 tablespoon sea salt

GARNISH
Flakey sea salt
Dill fronds
Puntarelle leaves

CHANTERELLES Finely dice mushrooms. Place in a bowl and combine with lemon juice, oil, and salt. The mushrooms will soften up and can be made into ovals, called quenelles, by using 2 spoons, 1 in each hand, to form the shapes. Start by dipping the spoons in hot water then take a spoonful of mushrooms and, using the other spoon, press into the quenelle.

CUCUMBER Finely dice cucumber and toss with dill, lemon zest, and salt.

DILL OIL Mix all ingredients in a high-speed blender. Strain through cheese cloth.

ASSEMBLY Place cucumber mixture in 3 different piles toward the center of each serving plate. Make 12 quenelles with the chanterelles and place 1 on top of each cucumber pile per plate. Spoon oil on top of each quenelle and sprinkle with a flakey sea salt. Garnish with dill fronds and puntarelle leaves.

Wild Mushrooms.
CORIANDER. FLAX SEED. CILANTRO.

This dish was on our first tasting menu at M.A.K.E. We wanted a nice, elegant version of a flatbread, and this is what we came up with. —SW

FLAX SEED CRISPS
- 1/2 cup roughly chopped celery
- 1/4 bunch fresh cilantro
- 1/4 cup coriander seeds
- 1 cup filtered water
- 1 cup golden flax seeds
- 1/2 cup whole brown flax seeds
- Pinch of sea salt

MUSHROOMS
- 1/4 cup olive oil
- 2 tablespoons elderberry liqueur (Saint Germaine)
- 1 tablespoon rice vinegar
- 1/2 teaspoon coriander seeds, ground
- 1/2 teaspoon fennel seeds, ground
- 1/4 teaspoon juniper berries, ground
- Pinch of sea salt
- 1 cup hen-of-the-woods mushrooms
- 1 cup oyster mushrooms
- 1 cup chanterelles

CORIANDER CREAM
- 1 cup cashews, soaked overnight
- 1/2 bunch cilantro, cleaned with stems
- 1 tablespoon coriander seeds
- 1 tablespoon rice vinegar
- 1 teaspoon lemon zest
- Pinch of sea salt

GARNISH
- Cilantro leaves
- Micro cilantro
- Cilantro flowers

FLAX SEED CRISPS Using a high-speed blender, blend celery, cilantro, coriander seeds, and water to combine. Pour into a large bowl and add flax seeds. Toss by hand to keep seeds whole. Add salt, to taste. Spread on teflex sheets and dehydrate at 115 degrees for about 2 hours or until you are able to peel off teflex. Peel and cut in 3- x 4-inch rectangles. Return to dehydrator on screens until completely dry and crisp, approximately 12 hours.

MUSHROOMS Combine oil, liqueur, vinegar, coriander, fennel, juniper berries, and salt in a large bowl to make a dressing. Toss mushrooms with dressing. Warm in dehydrator before serving.

CORIANDER CREAM Rinse and drain soaked nuts and place in a wide flat bowl. Using a smoking gun, smoke cashews by covering the bowl with plastic wrap and leaving the tube of the smoking gun inside. Smoke using hay or apple wood. Blend cashews with cilantro, coriander, vinegar, lemon zest, and salt until smooth in blender. It should be creamy but not runny.

ASSEMBLY Spread about 2 tablespoons Coriander Cream on each crisp. Remove mushrooms from the dehydrator and toss in a bowl. Top the cream with some mushrooms, making sure a mix of the different mushrooms will be in each bite. Garnish with cilantro leaves, micro cilantro, and cilantro flowers.

Herb Stems.
LEMON VERBENA CRÈME.
PORCINI CRACKER.

The lesson to be learned here is that stems are loaded with flavor, and once we know how to extract that flavor, they must be utilized. This is a great way to avoid throwing those precious resources out. —MK

PORCINI CRACKERS
1 cup almonds, soaked overnight
3/4 cup filtered water
1 1/2 tablespoons tamari
1 tablespoon porcini powder
1/2 teaspoon coriander
1 teaspoon agave nectar
1/4 cup flax seeds

LEMON VERBENA CREAM
1 cup cashews, soaked for 6 hours
1 cup lemon verbena leaves
1/4 cup filtered water
1 tablespoon lemon juice
1 teaspoon agave nectar
1/2 teaspoon sea salt

HERB STEMS
1/4 cup cilantro stems
1/4 cup parsley stems
1/4 cup mint stems
1/4 cup lovage stems
1/4 cup basil stems

PORCINI CRACKERS Mix all ingredients in a high-speed blender. Spread 1/4 inch thick on teflex sheets and dehydrate at 115 degrees for 4 hours. Punch out desired shape, such as 1 1/2-inch disks. Return to dehydrator on screens until completely dry and crisp, approximately 12 hours.

LEMON VERBENA CREAM Mix all ingredients in a high-speed blender. Pass through strainer to remove lumps, if any. Mixture should be thick but still spreadable.

HERB STEMS Remove all leaves from stems and save for another use. Slice stems into very small pieces. Mix all together.

ASSEMBLY Spread Lemon Verbena Cream on crackers. Top each with Herb Stems to completely cover the cream.

Morels.
PEA AVOCADO LEMON BALM.

Not only are these beautiful, but they are a vibrant, full-flavored raw version of stuffed mushrooms. They also happen to be addictive. —*MK*

MORELS
1/2 cup apple cider vinegar
1/4 cup agave nectar
1 tablespoon sea salt
12 morels, cleaned (each about 2–3 inches tall)

PEA AVOCADO LEMON BALM
1 ripe Hass avocado, peeled and seeded
1/2 cup English peas
1/2 cup lemon balm leaves
1/2 teaspoon sea salt

MORELS Mix vinegar, agave nectar, and salt together. Toss morels in brine and let sit for 1 hour.

PEA AVOCADO LEMON BALM Mix all ingredients in a high-speed blender.

ASSEMBLY Remove morels from brine. Place balm into an Isi syphon and charge with NO2. Using a small tip, inject balm into morels.

WE ARE OFTEN ASKED THE QUESTION. "How do you do what you do?" The answer is very simple and consists of three elements; we begin with the best ingredients, identify innovative techniques and equipment, and we dream. This first stage is the most important—identifying and using the best of everything. In LET, we allow the quality of the plants to speak for themselves . . . sometimes we need to just let things be. —*MK*

Let

Snap Peas.
HAZELNUT. MINT. LEMON ZEST.

Peas often get a bad rap for us when we're young as they definitely aren't good canned, are often overcooked, and also somehow end up in less than exciting dishes. However, look to Italy, and we can thank them for rustic preparations that allow this delicious little ingredient to speak for itself in all its sweet glory. —*MK*

LEMON HAZELNUT DRESSING
1/2 cup lemon juice, strained
1/4 cup hazelnut oil
1 teaspoon salt

SNAP PEAS
2 cups snap peas, deveined,*
   1 cup thinly sliced and
   1 cup opened up
1/2 cup pea shoots
1/2 cup mint leaves of different
   varieties (Vietnamese,
   chocolate, spearmint, etc.)

GARNISH
1 tablespoon lemon zest
1/4 cup grated hazelnuts
   (use a microplane)

LEMON HAZELNUT DRESSING Place the juice in a blender and add the oil and salt with the blender on the slowest setting. Blend to thoroughly combine.

ASSEMBLY Toss snap peas, pea shoots, and mint leaves in the dressing. Divide salad among serving plates and top with the lemon zest and hazelnuts.

Deveining snap peas is when you start from the tip of the snap pea and pull down the string that holds the peas in the pod. These "veins" are very fibrous and hard to chew.

Persimmon.
WILD ARUGULA. PISTACHIO.

This recipe really came together at the Santa Monica Farmers Market—the wild arugula from Maggie's Farm, the Santa Barbara pistachios and oil, and the wonderful persimmons that were all in perfect season at the time we put it on the menu. We let the farmers write our menus this way. —SW

I'm generally happy to see the seasons roll around, although this was my first experience with Scott's new style of salad, a signature plating format that we have since adopted throughout the company. I was not happy to see it fall off the menu when persimmons were no longer at the market. —MK

4 cups wild baby arugula
2 Fuyu persimmons, sliced

LEMON PISTACHIO
DRESSING
³/₄ cup olive oil
¹/₄ cup pistachio oil
¹/₂ cup lemon juice
1 tablespoon sea salt

PISTACHIO PURÉE
1 cup pistachios, soaked
 overnight
¹/₄ cup filtered water
1 tablespoon rice vinegar
1 tablespoon agave nectar
¹/₂ teaspoon salt

HACHIYA PURÉE
1 Hachiya persimmon, peeled
 and seeded
1 tablespoon lemon juice
1 teaspoon sea salt
¹/₄ cup olive oil

LEMON PISTACHIO DRESSING Using a blender, emulsify oils into lemon juice and salt at low speed.

PISTACHIO PURÉE Blend pistachios, water, vinegar, agave nectar, and salt in a high-speed blender until smooth. Pass through a strainer to remove any lumps.

HACHIYA PURÉE Place persimmon, lemon juice, and salt in a blender. Blend and add oil at low speed until smooth.

ASSEMBLY Toss arugula and Fuyu persimmons in Lemon Pistachio Dressing. Spoon a dollop of Pistachio Purée and Hachiya Purée on each plate and spread across the plates with a small offset spatula or the back of a spoon. Place the arugula and persimmons on top. Serve.

Radish. Sorrels.
MACADAMIA VINAIGRETTE.

I did not have a lot of radish in my life between when I was growing up and now. My parents loved them and they were a staple in our garden. Scott also seems to love them, and having them in this new context of raw cuisine is even more natural—if one can be addicted to texture, this may be the one. *—MK*

1 bunch French breakfast
  radishes
1 bunch Easter egg radishes
1 medium watermelon radish
1 bunch French sorrel
2 cups cleaned wood sorrel
  with 2-inch stems

2 cups radish or daikon
  sprouts
Coarse sea salt, to taste

MACADAMIA VINAIGRETTE
$1/2$ cup filtered water
$1/4$ cup macadamia nuts,
  soaked overnight

$1/4$ cup lemon juice
1 teaspoon sea salt
Zest from 1 lemon
$1/2$ cup macadamia oil

MACADAMIA VINAIGRETTE Place water, nuts, juice, salt, and zest in a high-speed blender. Blend and then emulsify oil using the slowest speed.

ASSEMBLY Slice and cut the radishes in different shapes and styles using a sheet slicer, mandolin, spiral slicer, or vegetable peeler. If the radishes come with the greens and they are clean and in good shape, use them as well in this salad.

Using 1 tablespoon of the Macadamia Vinaigrette per cup of radishes, toss vinaigrette and radishes to mix and then add the sorrels and sprouts. Toss to combine and add a sprinkle of salt. Place each serving in a big bowl or a wide flat plate.

Young Almond.
CUCUMBER. TARRAGON.

There are dishes that hit us over the head with flavor, or sneak up on us, and others are just calming with their simple elegance. This falls into that latter category—wonderful with a great glass of Chablis or sparkling wine. —*MK*

1 cucumber, sliced thin
   horizontally on a mandolin
1 cup young green almonds,
   peeled

TARRAGON OIL
1 cup fresh tarragon leaves
1/2 cup olive oil
1/2 tablespoon sea salt

SOUP STOCK
2 cups almond milk
1 cup cucumber juice*
1/2 teaspoon sea salt
1 pinch xanthan gum

GARNISH
1/2 cup tarragon leaves

TARRAGON OIL Mix all ingredients in a high-speed blender. Strain through cheese cloth.

SOUP STOCK Blend milk, juice, and salt. Strain through a chinois strainer 2 times. Add xanthan gum and blend again.

ASSEMBLY Place 2 slices of cucumber across the bottom of a bowl for each serving and add 8 to 9 almonds on top. Using a small squeeze bottle, drizzle tarragon oil on top of almonds. Evenly divide the soup among the bowls and garnish with a sprinkle of tarragon leaves. Serve.

Using an electric juicer, juice 1 large peeled cucumber for 1 cup juice.

Spring Vegetable Salad.
PISTACHIO. STRAWBERRY VINAIGRETTE.

We think of strawberries as a very sweet fruit, but they have a very nice tart character as well, which plays perfectly with vinegar and greens. —*MK*

SPRING VEGETABLES
4 cups baby mixed greens
1 cup sunflower sprouts
1 cup purslane, smaller tender
　leaves and stems
1 cup thinly sliced French
　breakfast radishes
1 cup shaved asparagus (use a
　vegetable peeler)

1 cup snap peas, deveined and
　split open*
1/4 cup mint leaves
1/4 cup basil leaves

PISTACHIO PURÉE
1 cup pistachios, soaked
　overnight
1/4 cup filtered water

1 tablespoon rice vinegar
1 tablespoon agave nectar
1/2 teaspoon sea salt

STRAWBERRY VINAIGRETTE
1 cup chopped strawberries
1 tablespoon rice vinegar
1 teaspoon sea salt
1/2 cup grapeseed oil

SPRING VEGETABLES Lightly toss all ingredients together in a large bowl.

PISTACHIO PURÉE Blend pistachios, water, vinegar, agave nectar, and salt in a high-speed blender until smooth. Pass through a strainer to remove any lumps.

STRAWBERRY VINAIGRETTE Place strawberries, vinegar, and salt in a blender. Blend until smooth. Emulsify oil into strawberry mix.

ASSEMBLY Place 1 tablespoon Pistachio Purée on each plate. Toss the Spring Vegetables with Strawberry Vinaigrette, reserving some vinaigrette for garnish. Evenly divide the salad among the plates, placing on top of the purée. Using a spoon or a squeeze bottle, drizzle more vinaigrette around the salad on the plate. Serve.

See page 27 for more information.

MANY APPLY SPROUTS to recipes for their fresh flavor and attractive appearance. Most even know that sprouts are packed with nutrients. Sprouts also are high in protein and are very easy to digest. They are in many ways a perfect food. —*MK*

Sprouted

Avocado. Radish.
NORI. SUNFLOWER. SPROUTS.

If there is one food that needs very little support, it would be the avocado. We just love this dish. —*MK*

2 Hass avocados, skins removed and cut into uniform pieces

4 Easter egg radishes, sliced

$^1/_4$ cup sunflower seeds

1 cup radish sprouts

Sea salt, to taste

1 cup nori, cut into strips

MISO LIME DRESSING

$^1/_4$ cup lime juice

1 tablespoon miso

Water

MISO LIME DRESSING Mix juice and miso together. Add just enough water to thin dressing, if needed. It should be a light, liquid consistency.

ASSEMBLY Evenly divide avocado among 4 plates and add radishes. Top with sunflower seeds and radish sprouts. Using a squeeze bottle, drizzle Miso Lime Dressing on salads. Top with a pinch of sea salt and nori strips.

Summer Roots
AND SHOOTS.

Root vegetables paired with sprouting vegetables brings together two dynamics, and in this example, with much success. The heavier roots benefit from the lighter, airy presence of the sprouts, and the visual results are just as compelling. —MK

ROOTS AND SHOOTS
2 large yellow carrots
1 tablespoon olive oil
1 teaspoon apple cider vinegar
Pinch of sea salt
6 baby carrots
2 baby candy cane beets
2 small radishes
4 asparagus

HERBED MACADAMIA
CHEESE
1 cup macadamia nuts, soaked
   overnight
1 tablespoon lemon juice
1 teaspoon lemon zest
1 tablespoon nutritional yeast
Pinch of sea salt
2 tablespoons minced tarragon

GARNISH
1/2 cup mixed micro herbs or
   small leaves of herbs (mint,
   basil, cilantro, etc.)

ROOTS AND SHOOTS Slice large yellow carrots lengthwise on a mandolin on the widest setting. Toss with oil, vinegar, and salt. Remove carrots from dressing and place in a vacuum bag. Seal at 100 percent to marinate and compress carrots. Slice the rest of vegetables vertically and toss in the dressing.

HERBED MACADAMIA CHEESE Add macadamia nuts, lemon juice, zest, nutritional yeast, and salt to a food processor. Pulse until fluffy and creamy. Fold in tarragon.

ASSEMBLY Lay a large carrot slice on each serving plate, and using a pastry bag, dollop macadamia cheese randomly on top of carrot. Place some of the remaining vegetables on top of the carrots and garnish nicely with micro herbs. Sprinkle sea salt on top.

Fennel. Beets.
RADISH. SORREL.

If you think about it, red and white plants are very dynamic together, sweet versus mostly bitter. In this dish, sorrel adds not only an earthy contrast, but also subtle hints of strawberry and kiwi—just enough to elevate a classic combination to something unique and new. —MK

SALAD
1 small chioggia beet
1 small golden beet
2 spring radishes
1 large fennel bulb
1 tablespoon lemon juice
2 tablespoons olive oil

Pinch of sea salt
1 cup red-veined sorrel leaves

SORREL CREAM DRESSING
8 sorrel leaves
$1/2$ cup cashews, soaked
    overnight

$1/4$ cup water
1 tablespoon lemon juice
Zest from 1 lemon
Sea salt

GARNISH
Fennel fronds

SALAD Thinly slice beets, radishes, and fennel using a mandolin. Slice the beets vertically from top to bottom. Add all to a bowl and toss with a dressing made out of the lemon juice, oil, and salt. Add sorrel leaves and lightly toss together.

SORREL CREAM DRESSING Add all ingredients to a high-speed blender. Blend until completely smooth. Add more water, if needed. Pass through a strainer.

ASSEMBLY Arrange beets, radishes, and fennel in the center of each plate. Build it by placing the vegetables so you can see the different colors. Drizzle sorrel cream around the salad on the plates. Garnish with fennel fronds.

Sword Leaf. Coconut.
CURRY CASHEW. CARROT. RADISH.
APPLE.

SERVES 6

On my first visit to the Santa Monica Farmers Market, I was introduced to the Sword Leaf. I was immediately attracted by its slender and pointed shape then I was told to try it by Clarita from Coleman Farms. I tore off a piece and gave it a try. At first, it is similar Romaine and then there is a familiar earthy taste. Basmati rice! I knew I had to use some curry flavors with my new discovery. —SW

SALAD
4 medium heads sword leaf lettuce or romaine hearts
2 cups scarlet frill or purple mustard greens
$1/2$ cup currants
Pinch of salt

COCONUT DRESSING
$1/4$ cup rice vinegar
$1/2$ tablespoon agave nectar
$1/2$ teaspoon fennel seeds
$1/2$ teaspoon ground cardamom
$1/2$ teaspoon sea salt
$1/2$ cup coconut oil

CURRY CASHEWS
1 tablespoon coconut sugar
1 tablespoon curry powder
$1/2$ teaspoon sea salt
1 tablespoon water
1 cup cashews

CARROT PURÉE
1 cup peeled and chopped carrots
$1/4$ cup carrot juice*
$1/4$ cup cashews, soaked for 1 hour
$1/2$ teaspoon curry powder
1 teaspoon agave nectar
1 teaspoon minced peeled ginger

$1/2$ Thai chile, seeded and minced
$1/4$ teaspoon sea salt
$1/4$ cup olive oil

RADISHES AND APPLES
1 large watermelon or daikon radish
1 apple

SALAD Add sword leaf, mustard greens, currants, and salt to a large bowl; toss.

COCONUT DRESSING Place vinegar, agave nectar, fennel, cardamom, and salt into a high-speed blender and blend to combine. Add coconut oil and blend at the slowest speed to emulsify.

continued

Sword Leaf ... continued

CURRY CASHEWS Mix coconut sugar, curry powder, salt, and water in a bowl. Add cashews and stir to combine. Spread cashews on a dehydrator sheet and dehydrate at 115 degrees for 10 hours or until completely dry.

CARROT PURÉE Using a high-speed blender, blend all ingredients except the oil until smooth. Drizzle in oil while machine is running at slowest speed to emulsify. Pass through a strainer.

RADISHES AND APPLES Using a small melon baller make as many balls from the radish and apple as you can.

ASSEMBLY Toss Salad with half the dressing, adding more if needed. Spread about a tablespoon of Carrot Purée across each serving plate with an offset spatula. Then arrange a good handful of dressed salad greens on top. Evenly divide radish and apple balls among servings and sprinkle with cashews.

Using an electric juicer, juice 2 medium carrots for $^1/_4$ cup carrot juice.

Shaved Sunchoke.
SUNFLOWER SPROUTS. SEEDS AND OIL.

Sunchokes and sunflowers are in the same family. I thought it would be fun to use the cousins together and make a nice starter. —*SW*

1 tablespoon lemon juice	6 sunchokes, cleaned and	¹/₂ cup sunflower seeds
2 tablespoons sunflower oil	peeled	
Pinch of sea salt	2 cups sunflower sprouts	

Make a quick dressing by stirring together the lemon juice, sunflower oil, and salt.

Thinly slice sunchokes lengthwise using a mandolin and toss in dressing. Remove sunchokes from dressing and toss sunflower sprouts with dressing.

TO SERVE Divide the sunchokes evenly between serving plates, placing them flat on the plates. Sprinkle the seeds on top of sunchokes and place sprouts in a nice pile on top of both.

I'LL ADMIT IT. Soups are not my favorite food, and yet, in the raw food world, I have learned to love them. Classically, they too often cross the boundary between soup and stew, flavors become unbalanced after reduction, and the variables are just too great to properly calibrate consistency. However, utilizing juices, essences, and vegetable stocks with natural thickening agents can yield remarkable, satisfying results, which we're happy to share in this chapter. —MK

Spun

Bartlett Pear Soup.
YOUNG CELERY. JUNIPER OIL.

Scott has a way with elegant, almost poetic combinations that defy gravity in a sense. This soup is so light and ethereal that you wonder how it can satisfy, and yet it does, in a most earthy fashion. —MK

JUNIPER OIL
1/2 cup juniper berries
1 cup olive oil

SOUP
1 quart almond milk
2 cups pear juice

2 cups celery juice*
1 teaspoon salt
1 teaspoon xanthan gum
1 cup diced Bartlett pear
1/2 cup diced young celery
   stems

GARNISH
Micro sorrel
Borage flowers

JUNIPER OIL Blend juniper berries and oil. Let blended mixture sit for at least 48 hours. Strain through chinois strainer 2 times.

SOUP Blend milk, juices, and salt together. Strain through a chinois strainer 2 times. Add xanthan and blend again. Adjust with additional salt, if necessary.

ASSEMBLY Place a tablespoon of the pear and a teaspoon of the celery stems in the center of each serving bowl. Spoon Juniper Oil on top of pear and celery. Pour soup over top and garnish with the sorrel and borage flowers.

Using an electric juicer, juice 16 stalks of celery for 2 cups celery juice.

Carrot Soup.
RADISH. CHILE OIL. CARROT CLOUD.

As the saying goes, we eat with our eyes first. Even if you never taste this, you'll love it! It's a visual and flavorful wonder—rich, sweet, bitter, spicy, and well rounded. *—MK*

ALMOND SHALLOT MILK
1 cup almonds, soaked
   overnight
1/4 cup chopped shallots
1 teaspoon sea salt
3 cups filtered water

CARROT RADISH SALAD
1 cup peeled and diced carrots
1/2 cup diced daikon radish
1/2 cup diced watermelon
   radish

1/2 cup peeled and diced
   Granny Smith apple
1/2 cup peeled and diced
   cucumber
1 teaspoon apple cider vinegar
Pinch of sea salt

CARROT SOUP
5 cups fresh carrot juice
3 cups almond shallot milk
1/4 cup lemon juice
1/4 cup olive oil
1 tablespoon sea salt

CHILE OIL
1 cup olive oil
12 Thai chiles, stems removed
1 jalapeño, stem removed
2 stalks lemongrass, peeled
   and chopped
1 cup cilantro leaves
1 tablespoon salt
1 tablespoon agave nectar

ALMOND SHALLOT MILK Blend all ingredients. Strain through nut milk bag.

CARROT RADISH SALAD Toss all the ingredients together in a bowl.

CARROT SOUP Combine all ingredients in blender and blend until smooth. Strain through chinois strainer 2 times, saving the foam.

CHILE OIL Combine all ingredients in blender and blend until smooth. Strain through chinois strainer.

ASSEMBLY Make a ring mold of the salad in 6 serving bowls. Spoon 1 tablespoon Chile Oil over each salad. Top with a carrot "cloud." The cloud is a natural foam that happens when the soup is spun in a high-speed blender. Pour soup into the bowls around but not over the salad.

Green and Ripe Strawberries.
CITRUS PIGNOLI YOGURT. DILL.

Green strawberries are unripe strawberries and are definitely tart. Dehydrating them enhances that tartness and adds texture, making for an exciting flavor burst.

CITRUS PIGNOLI YOGURT
2 cups pine nuts
1 probiotic capsule
$1/2$ cup water
1 tablespoon lemon juice
Pinch of sea salt
1 tablespoon lemon zest
1 tablespoon chopped
   fresh dill

STRAWBERRY BROTH
2 cups ripe strawberries, sliced
   in half
2 cups filtered water
1 tablespoon balsamic vinegar
1 tablespoon chickpea miso
$1/2$ teaspoon toasted
   sesame oil
$1/2$ teaspoon sea salt

GREEN STRAWBERRIES
24 green strawberries

GARNISH
Fresh dill fronds

CITRUS PIGNOLI YOGURT Blend pine nuts and probiotic capsule, adding water to get a yogurt like consistency. Let sit on a shelf, covered, for 8–12 hours (overnight). Blend again, and season with lemon juice and salt. Fold in lemon zest and dill by hand.

STRAWBERRY BROTH Add all ingredients to a high-speed blender. Blend on high for 90 seconds. Strain through chinois strainer at least 2 times.

GREEN STRAWBERRIES Thinly slice strawberries and dehydrate at 115 degrees for 6 hours or until dry.

ASSEMBLY Place 1 tablespoon yogurt on the bottom of a shallow bowl for each serving. Top the yogurt with green strawberries and a sprinkling of dill fronds. Pour the Strawberry Broth tableside.

Shiitake. Paprika Broth.
GREEN TOMATO. BABY CORN. CILANTRO.

The flavor of this dish was inspired by the flavors of summer. Even though we typically associate shiitake with Asian flavors, it adds a rustic undertone to this dish that combines well with the sweet corn and smoky paprika. —*MK*

DRESSING
2 tablespoon lime juice
2 tablespoons olive oil
$1/2$ teaspoon chili powder
Pinch of sea salt

VEGETABLES
18–20 ears baby corn, sliced in half, from top to bottom

4 medium green tomatoes, cut into $1/2$-inch slices
1 cup small shiitake mushrooms, tops 1 inch wide (stems reserved, dehydrated, and blended into a powder using a high-speed blender)
1 cup cilantro leaves, stems saved and chopped

PAPRIKA BROTH
2 cups filtered water
$1/2$ cup chopped red bell pepper
$1/4$ cup shiitake stem powder
2 tablespoons sweet paprika
1 tablespoon hot smoked paprika
1 tablespoon tamari

DRESSING Make dressing by whisking the lime juice, oil, chili powder, and sea salt together.

VEGETABLES Toss corn in dressing and let sit for 5 minutes. Toss in tomatoes, mushrooms, and chopped cilantro stems.

PAPRIKA BROTH Heat the water as hot as you would like and add to a high-speed blender along with all of the other ingredients. Blend on high for 90 seconds. Strain through a chinois strainer at least 2 times. Serve warm. (You can keep warm covered in a dehydrator set to 145 degrees, but be careful not to dehydrate it away. It shouldn't stay in the dehydrator for very long.)

ASSEMBLY Carefully scatter the vegetables in the bottom of each serving bowl. Lay cilantro leaves on top. Serve broth by pouring tableside.

EARLY RAW FOOD PRIMARILY APPLIED DEHYDRATION when preparing crackers, breads, crusts, or other components. Today, those are only part of what we rely on this essential technique for. The dehydrator is also perfect for concentrating flavor, infusing oils, reducing sauces and dressings, or even just warming a dish. It would be hard to imagine raw food being where it is today without this key process. —MK

Dried

Radishes.
RYE SEAWEED CRISPS.
MACADAMIA BUTTERS.

Those of us who enjoy a great French bistro may have had radishes and butter. I can't say for sure, as I haven't asked, but I assume Scott had that in mind when creating this. It also happens to the first thing I reach for when I arrive at M.A.K.E., particularly the Macadamia Butter. It has a haunting richness I never tire of. —*MK*

RADISH SALAD
1 bunch radishes, cleaned
1 cup radish sprouts
2 tablespoons macadamia
　　nut oil
Pinch of sea salt

RYE SEAWEED CRISPS
1 cup celery juice*
1 cup rye flour
$1/2$ cup dulse
$1/2$ cup water
$1/2$ cup flax meal
1 tablespoon kombu powder
1 sheet nori
$1/2$ teaspoon sea salt

SMOKED MACADAMIA
BUTTER
1 cup macadamia nuts, soaked
　　overnight
1 cup water
1 tablespoon mushroom
　　powder
1 teaspoon nutritional yeast
$1/2$ teaspoon sea salt

CAPER MACADAMIA
BUTTER
1 cup macadamia nuts, soaked
　　overnight
$1/2$ cup water
1 tablespoon finely chopped
　　capers
1 tablespoon mushroom
　　powder

1 teaspoon nutritional yeast
$1/2$ teaspoon sea salt

COCONUT BACON
$1/4$ chipotle chile, seeded and
　　soaked in 1 cup filtered
　　water for 10 minutes
$1/2$ cup soaking water from the
　　chipotle pepper
$1/4$ cup maple syrup
1 tablespoon cumin
1 tablespoon olive oil
1 tablespoon tamari
1 teaspoon apple cider vinegar
1 teaspoon sea salt
1 teaspoon smoked paprika
1 tablespoon mesquite
2 cups coconut flakes

RADISH SALAD Slice radishes lengthwise in quarters or eighths, depending how big they are. Place in a bowl and toss with sprouts, macadamia oil, and salt.

continued

Radishes ... continued

RYE SEAWEED CRISPS Blend together all ingredients and spread about $1/8$ inch thick on a nonstick dehydrator sheet. Dehydrate at 115 degrees for 12 hours or until crisp.

SMOKED MACADAMIA BUTTER Blend all ingredients until extremely smooth. Smoke with smoking gun using hay or apple wood. Place the emulsion in a bowl, cover it with a lid or plastic wrap, and leave the smoking tube inside the bowl. Let smoke set covered in bowl for about 10 minutes.

CAPER MACADAMIA BUTTER Blend all until extremely smooth. Fold in capers.

COCONUT BACON Blend all ingredients except for coconut in a blender until smooth. Combine with coconut flakes in a bowl and then spread evenly in a thin layer on a nonstick dehydrator sheet. Dehydrate at 115 degrees for 8–10 hours or until crispy throughout.

ASSEMBLY Using 2 ramekins per serving, place some Smoked Macadamia Butter in 1 and some Caper Macadamia Butter in the other. Top the Smoked Macadamia with some crumbled Coconut Bacon. Equally divide the radish salad among serving plates and add the ramekins on the side. Break rye crisps to the size you like and serve. Alternately, if you are serving a group or family style, place the butters in separate bowls, equally divide the salad and place on top of the butters, and serve with the crisps.

Using an electric juicer, juice 8 stalks of celery for 1 cup celery juice.

Pumpkin Gnocchi.
WATERCRESS. APPLE CIDER.

This happens to be one of those perfectly engineered dishes that most anyone would love, regardless of their experience with raw cuisine. The cider component really finishes this, both from a creative and a flavor viewpoint. —*MK*

GNOCCHI
2 cups peeled and chopped
    butternut squash
2 cups peeled and chopped
    jicama
2 1/2 cups cashews, soaked for
    4 hours or more
1/4 cup coconut meat
1/4 cup nutritional yeast
1/4 cup olive oil
1/2 teaspoon sea salt
1 tablespoon minced fresh
    thyme

1 tablespoon minced flat-leaf
    parsley

WATERCRESS PURÉE
1/2 bunch watercress
1/2 teaspoon sea salt
1/2 cup olive oil

CIDER SAUCE
1 cup apple juice
12 sprigs thyme
1/2 cup apple cider vinegar

1 teaspoon agave nectar
1/4 teaspoon sea salt

PICKLED APPLES
1 large Granny Smith apple,
    peeled and diced
1 tablespoon apple cider
    vinegar
Pinch of sea salt

GARNISH
Watercress

GNOCCHI Pulse squash and jicama in a high-speed blender until smooth. Strain excess water from the pulp. Blend pulp with the cashews, coconut, nutritional yeast, oil, and salt until smooth. Fold the thyme and parsley into batter. Form into 1 1/2-inch gnocchi shapes and dehydrate at 115 degrees for 6 hours.

WATERCRESS PURÉE In a food processor, pulse the watercress and salt until it is a purée. Slowly add the oil while the processor is in motion to thoroughly blend. Pass through a strainer.

CIDER SAUCE Reduce apple juice with thyme sprigs in dehydrator at 115 degrees overnight or until reduced by half. Remove the thyme and blend with vinegar, agave nectar, and salt in a blender until smooth and creamy.

PICKLED APPLES Place apple in a bowl and toss with vinegar and salt. Place in a vacuum bag and seal at 100 percent. After the bag has been sealed, it is ready to serve right away.

ASSEMBLY Spoon Cider Sauce in a circle on each plate. Then spoon Watercress Purée in separate circle. Place 5 to 7 gnocchi randomly on the plate on top of and inside the circles of sauce. Add 1 piece of apple to each gnocchi. Garnish with watercress.

Carrot Gnocchi.
PEAS. MINT. HORSERADISH CRUMBS.

Clever. I don't often think of our cuisine as cute, but this is right on the border of cute while carrying elegant flavor and just bringing a hint of springtime. —MK

The classic combo of peas and carrots definitely calls spring to mind. —SW

GNOCCHI
1/2 cup peeled and chopped jicama
2 cups peeled and chopped carrots
1 1/2 cups cashews, soaked for at least 4 hours
1 teaspoon olive oil
1 teaspoon agave nectar
1/2 teaspoon sea salt

1 tablespoon chopped parsley
1 teaspoon chopped thyme

PEA MINT PESTO
2 cups frozen peas
2 cups fresh pea leaves, reserve tendrils
1 cup mint leaves
1/4 teaspoon sea salt
1/2 cup olive oil

HORSERADISH FLAX CRUMBS
1 cup flax seeds
1/2 cup peeled and chopped horseradish
1/2 cup water
1 teaspoon salt

GNOCCHI Pulse the jicama in a high-speed blender until it is smooth. Strain any excess water from the pulp. Blend carrots into a pulp. Combine the carrot pulp with the jicama pulp and blend with the remaining ingredients until smooth. Form into 1 1/2-inch gnocchi shapes and dehydrate at 115 degrees for 6–8 hours.

PEA MINT PESTO In a food processor, pulse peas, pea leaves, mint leaves, and salt until it forms a purée. Slowly add in the oil while the processor is in motion to thoroughly blend.

HORSERADISH FLAX CRUMBS Using a high-speed blender, blend all ingredients until well combined. Spread on a nonstick dehydrator sheet and dehydrate at 115 degrees for 12 hours or until crisp. Break into rough pieces.

ASSEMBLY Spoon about 2 tablespoons of Pea Mint Pesto onto each serving plate and press down. If you want to be neat, you can use a ring mold to make a nice circle shape. Take the gnocchi and stick some pea tendrils in one end of each so that the gnocchi look like they have carrot tops. Place 5 to 7 gnocchi randomly on top of the pesto. Place horseradish crisps into pesto next to gnocchi. Serve.

Sweet Potato Chips.
BLACK PEPPER CREAM. HIJIKI CAVIAR.

SERVES 8

We've worked for years to find the right formula for a raw food chip and here it is. It's great with anything but works as a perfect amuse. —MK

SWEET POTATO CHIPS
1 medium sweet potato
1 tablespoon olive oil
1 teaspoon sea salt

BLACK PEPPER CREAM
1 cup cashews, soaked
   overnight

$^3/_4$ cup filtered water
$^1/_2$ tablespoon black
   peppercorns
$^1/_4$ cup lemon juice
1 tablespoon nutritional yeast
1 teaspoon sea salt

HIJIKI CAVIAR
$^1/_4$ cup hijiki
2 tablespoons rice vinegar
1 teaspoon lemon juice
1 teaspoon agave nectar
1 teaspoon salt

SWEET POTATO CHIPS Slice sweet potato into very thin, almost translucent, rounds. Rinse in a large bowl of water. Drain and repeat rinse 3 times. Toss sweet potato chips with oil and salt. Place chips on mesh screens and sprinkle salt over the chips again. Dehydrate at 118 degrees for 1 day or until crispy and dry.

BLACK PEPPER CREAM Using a high-speed blender, blend all ingredients until smooth. Taste and adjust seasonings, if needed.

HIJIKI CAVIAR Soak the hijiki in cold water for 1 hour. Drain well and place the hijiki in the bowl of a food processor. Pulse until the hijiki is broken down into caviar-size bits. Transfer to a bowl and add the vinegar, lemon juice, agave nectar, and salt. Stir well and cover. Let the caviar marinate for 1 hour in the refrigerator. Strain off any excess liquid.

ASSEMBLY Place Sweet Potato Chips flat on a serving platter. Fill a squeeze bottle with Black Pepper Cream and squeeze cream onto the chips. Spoon about $^1/_4$ teaspoon of Hijiki Caviar onto each dollop of cream and serve.

Zucchini Hummus.
MUHAMMARA. SESAME TABBOULEH.
ZA'ATAR CRACKERS.

SERVES 6–8

I've been a huge fan of Mediterranean cuisine for most of my adult life—Scott's variations are a bit lighter than our earlier versions, and this has simply become one of our most popular sharing dishes. —MK

ZUCCHINI ALMOND HUMMUS
2 cups peeled and chopped zucchini
1 1/2 cups almonds, soaked overnight
1 cup tahini
1/4 cup olive oil
1/4 cup lemon juice
1 teaspoon salt
2 teaspoons cumin
1 large clove garlic

MUHAMMARA
4 red bell peppers, seeded
1 tablespoon olive oil
Pinch of salt
3 cups walnuts, finely chopped
2 tablespoons fresh lemon juice, or to taste
1 tablespoons agave nectar
1 teaspoon cumin
1/2 teaspoon dried hot red pepper flakes
1/2 teaspoon salt
3/4 cup extra virgin olive oil

SESAME TABBOULEH
1/2 cup white sesame seeds
1/4 cup olive oil
2 tablespoons lemon juice
1 tablespoon sea salt
1 cup peeled, seeded, and 1/4-inch diced cucumber
1 cup seeded and 1/4-inch diced Roma tomato
1 cup flat-leaf parsley, chopped
1/2 cup basil leaves, chopped
1/2 cup mint leaves, chopped

GARNISH
Za'atar Crackers

ZUCCHINI ALMOND HUMMUS Pulse all ingredients together in a food processor until smooth. Adjust seasoning, as needed.

MUHAMMARA Toss bell peppers in olive oil with a pinch of salt and place on dehydrator tray. Dehydrate at 115 degrees for 1 hour. Then finely dice and set aside.

Using a food processor, blend together walnuts, lemon juice, agave nectar, cumin, red pepper flakes, and salt until mixture is smooth. With the motor running, gradually add the extra virgin olive oil. Stir in the bell peppers. Transfer the Muhammara to a bowl and serve at room temperature.

SESAME TABBOULEH Toss all ingredients in a bowl until well combined.

ASSEMBLY The best way to serve this is to share. Spoon tabbouleh, hummus, and Muhammara into bowls and randomly place Za'atar Crackers standing up in the different dips.

Radicchio.
AVOCADO. CITRUS. NORI. HEMP. OLIVE.

Radicchio has evolved from one of the most overused products to being underappreciated. In the 90s, every restaurant seemed to have a tricolor salad, which was pretty simple and not exciting. Yet, when radicchio's richness is paired with a healthy fat, or a couple of them, it creates a symphony. Add the punch of these dynamic black olives and you have dish that just sparkles. —*MK*

SALAD
2 small radicchio
1 avocado
2 white grapefruit, cut into
    segments
1 cup raw nori, cut in to strips

HEMP OIL POWDER
1/2 cup tapioca maltodextrin*
1 tablespoon hemp oil

CITRUS VINAIGRETTE
1/2 cup lemon juice

1/2 cup olive oil
Pinch of sea salt

BLACK OLIVE CRUMBS
1/2 cup pitted whole
    black olives

SALAD Cut radicchio vertically into 8 pieces, letting the core hold the leaves together. Peel the avocado and dice.

HEMP OIL POWDER Place tapioca in a food processor. Add oil while pulsing the powder in the processor. You may have to add more powder if it is too wet. Gradually add more powder, starting with a tablespoon. Pass through a strainer to enhance the fluffiness.

CITRUS VINAIGRETTE Blend lemon juice, oil, and salt together until emulsified.

BLACK OLIVE CRUMBS Place olives on dehydrator tray and dehydrate at 115 degrees for 24 hours or until crispy. Place dried olives in a food processor and pulse until olives become crumbly.

ASSEMBLY This salad is fun to serve family style. Toss radicchio and avocado in a large bowl with about half of the dressing, using more if needed. Spoon a few tablespoons of the Hemp Oil Powder over the salad and add the grapefruit segments and olive crumbs. Top with the nori and serve.

See page 157 for more information.

WHEN WE LEARNED that a company we work with, PolyScience, sells something called a smoking gun, we couldn't resist. This is a brilliant tool, and not terribly expensive. It is used to impart a smoky flavor to food and is much easier to control than other smoking methods. It is also incredibly useful for richer elements of a dish that have a bit of fat and body. Although we apply it subtly, smoked foods are a mainstay of all our menus these days. —MK

Smoked

Coriander Toast.
SMOKED CASHEWS. HERBS. FLOWERS.

Smoking is especially well received when utilized for a first flavor, or an amuse. It's a surprise that leads the palate on a journey and opens the mind to the creative meal ahead. *—MK*

CORIANDER TOAST
1/2 cup golden flax seeds
1 cup almonds, soaked overnight
1 cup water
2 tablespoons tamari
1 tablespoon agave nectar
2 tablespoons freshly ground coriander seeds

SMOKED CASHEWS
2 cups cashews, soaked overnight
1 tablespoon apple cider vinegar
1 teaspoon smoked paprika
2 teaspoons sea salt
1/2 cup water

GARNISH
2 cups mixed micro herbs
Edible flowers, of choice

CORIANDER TOAST Grind half of the flax seeds; set aside. Mix almonds, water, tamari, agave nectar, and coriander seeds in a high-speed blender until it becomes a paste. Fold in whole and ground flax seeds. Let set for 10 minutes.

Spread a thin layer, 1/8–1/4 inch thick, on teflex sheets and score into 2- x 3 1/2-inch pieces. Dehydrate at 115 degrees for 4 hours. Remove from teflex sheets and finish dehydrating on screens for another 6–8 hours until dry.

SMOKED CASHEWS Blend all ingredients in a high-speed blender until smooth and creamy. Smoke the cashew emulsion with a smoking gun using hay or apple wood. Place the emulsion in a bowl, cover it with a lid or plastic wrap, and leave the smoking tube inside the bowl. Let smoke sit covered in bowl for about 10 minutes.

ASSEMBLY Spread cashew emulsion generously on coriander toasts and garnish with mixed micro herbs and flowers.

Smoked Sea Vegetables.
PICKLED DAIKON. LEMONGRASS.

A good dish is often referred to as a great dish if it achieves umami and reaches all of our taste senses. Simply thinking about smoky sea vegetables evokes a deep, haunting flavor that speaks volumes about the impact this dish has as part of a meal. —MK

SMOKED SEA VEGETABLE BROTH
10 cups hot filtered water
2 leaves kombu
1/2 cup dulse
1/2 cup dried hijiki
2 stalks lemongrass, thinly sliced
1 tablespoon chickpea miso
1 tablespoon tamari
1 tablespoon lime juice
1/2 teaspoon toasted sesame oil

FLOWER CHOY
1 bunch flowering choy (baby bok choy can be substituted)
Zest from 1 lemon
1 teaspoon toasted sesame oil
Pinch of sea salt

PICKLED DAIKON
1 bunch baby daikon or icicle radishes (regular daikon thinly cut can be used)
1 stalk lemongrass
2 tablespoons rice vinegar
1 tablespoon agave nectar
1 teaspoon sea salt

SMOKED SEA VEGETABLE BROTH Make a tea using the water, kombu, dulse, hijiki, and lemongrass. Place in a pitcher or large jar, cover, and let set for at least 1 hour. Strain and save the kombu and hijiki. Discard the dulse and lemongrass. Stir the tamari, lime juice, and sesame oil into the broth and set aside.

Rinse kombu and hijiki. Slice kombu into thin noodle-like strips and toss with hijiki. Using a smoking gun, smoke seaweed with hay or apple wood. Place seaweed in a bowl, cover it with a lid or plastic wrap, and leave the smoking tube inside the bowl. Let set covered in bowl for about 10 minutes. Set aside.

FLOWER CHOY Clean choy greens and trim so the choy will be close to the same length. Place in a bowl and toss with lemon zest, sesame oil, and salt.

PICKLED DAIKON Clean daikon and bruise lemongrass by lightly pounding it with the back end of a cleaver or chef's knife then roughly mince. In a bowl, whisk together vinegar, agave nectar, and salt. Toss in the lemongrass and then the daikon. Place all in a vacuum bag and seal at 100 percent. Let pickles set for at least 4 hours at room temperature. Refrigerate after opening the vacuum bag.

ASSEMBLY In deep serving bowls, place daikon, choy, and seaweed in the bottom but leaning up and to the side. Pour in broth and serve.

Smoked Heirloom Tomato.
WHITE PEACHES. BASIL ICE.

Not surprisingly, this is all about summer. Find the best tomatoes. Find the ripest peaches. Prepare and enjoy. —*MK*

1 cup small leaves mixed basil,
(Thai, lemon, bush, opal,
sweet, cinnamon, etc.),
rinsed

2 white peaches, sliced

SMOKED TOMATOES
4 medium heirloom tomatoes
1 tablespoon olive oil
Sprinkle of salt

BASIL ICE
1 cup basil juice*
1/2 teaspoon sea salt
1/4 cup olive oil

SMOKED TOMATOES Slice tomatoes into wedges and toss lightly with the olive oil and salt. Using the smoking gun, smoke the tomatoes with peach wood. Place the tomatoes in a bowl, cover it with a lid or plastic wrap, and leave the smoking tube inside the bowl. Let smoke set covered in bowl for about 10 minutes.

BASIL ICE Place basil juice and salt into a blender and emulsify oil to combine.

Line a sheet pan with sides with plastic wrap. Pour basil oil evenly onto plastic wrap and freeze. When frozen, break into chip-like pieces and keep frozen until time to serve.

ASSEMBLY Place some basil ice on each serving plate. Toss tomatoes and peaches with basil and arrange on top of ice. As ice melts, it becomes an amazing dressing.

Using an electric juicer, juice 1 pound basil for 1 cup juice.

Smoked Cherries.
WATERCRESS. RADISHES. JICAMA.
GINGER LIME. SPICED PEPITAS.

In my opinion, cherries belong in salads, with arugula, watercress, or anything with a touch of bitterness. I tend to add avocado to everything, so you may want to think about that as well. —*MK*

SALAD
1 bunch watercress
1 cup sliced radishes, (vertical thin slices using a mandolin)
1/2 cup diced jicama

SMOKED CHERRIES
2 cups cherries, halved and seeded
1 tablespoon olive oil
Sprinkle of salt

VINAIGRETTE
1/2 cup olive oil
1/4 cup fresh lime juice
1/4 cup ginger, peeled and chopped
1 tablespoon agave nectar
1/2 teaspoon salt
1/4 cup fresh cilantro leaves and stems
2 tablespoons fresh parsley

SPICED PEPITAS
1 cup raw pumpkin seeds
1/4 cup maple syrup
1 tablespoon tamari
1/2 teaspoon ginger powder
1/4 teaspoon cayenne pepper

SALAD Rinse the watercress and spin dry. Mix the watercress with radishes and jicama in a large bowl.

SMOKED CHERRIES Toss cherries lightly with the oil and salt. Using the smoking gun, smoke the cherries with cherry wood. Place the cherries in a bowl, cover it with a lid or plastic wrap, and leave the smoking tube inside the bowl. Let smoke set covered in bowl for about 10 minutes.

VINAIGRETTE Blend oil, lime juice, ginger, agave nectar, and salt in a high-speed blender until smooth. Add cilantro and parsley and blend until well combined and completely smooth.

SPICED PEPITAS Mix all ingredients and spread on dehydrator sheets. Dehydrate at 115 degrees for 12 hours or until dry.

ASSEMBLY Toss Salad with Vinaigrette using about 1/2 cup, adding more if needed. When dressed to your liking, serve on individual plates or in shallow bowls. Top with Smoked Cherries and a sprinkle of pepitas.

PREPARING PLANT-BASED FOODS utilizing both a vacuum seal and a sous vide machine are ways of increasing flavor without losing moisture, thus achieving a more pleasing texture. The sealing method provides an even flavor and can be used on virtually any ingredient. The thermal immersion circulators, sous vide machines, concentrate flavors and lightly "cook" ingredients that need tenderizing by maintaining a constant temperature. This method is one of the most accurate forms of food preparation and is invaluable when working with root vegetables, mushrooms, and other foods that are better when tender and intensely flavorful. *—MK*

Sealed

Buna Shimeji Mushrooms.
CAPERBERRIES. ALMOND. ORANGE.

This is a recipe ideal for small portions, or as an amuse. It nearly achieves umami, as the nutty mushroom counterbalances with it's tart and briny partners. —MK

1/2 cup orange juice	1 cup buna shimeji mushrooms	2 cara cara oranges, supremed*
1/4 cup almond oil	12 sprigs thyme	2 tablespoons slivered almonds
1 tablespoon caperberry brine	12 caperberries, sliced thin horizontally	Edible flowers
1/4 teaspoon sea salt		

Make a dressing by whisking orange juice, oil, caperberry brine, and salt together in a small bowl.

Toss mushrooms in this dressing and then remove. Strain and reserve dressing. Place mushrooms in a vacuum bag with thyme sprigs and seal at 100 percent. Place in a sous vide water bath at 115 degrees for 90 minutes.

ASSEMBLY Remove mushrooms from sealed bag and discard thyme. Spoon a tablespoon of the dressing in the bottom of small shallow serving bowls. Place 3 orange segments on top of dressing and lay 1 mushroom on each orange segment. Then place a slivered almond and a sliced caperberry on top of that. Garnish with a flower on each as well.

Supreming a citrus fruit is when the skin is cut away from the fruit and the segments are cut out. Always cut the segments from the fruit over a bowl so you save the juices.

King Oyster.
WATERCRESS. APRICOT.
ESPELETTE PEPPER.

One of my first lessons utilizing sous vide for raw food was with portobello mushrooms. While I always loved them prepared in a dehydrator, it was not until we prepared them using the sous vide method that we achieved the same flavor without all the moisture loss. While we are not trying to achieve a meat replica, the meaty texture appeals to many who miss that when converting to a plant-based diet. King oyster mushrooms do the same. —MK

KING OYSTERS
6 king oyster mushrooms
1/2 cup olive oil
1/2 cup sherry vinegar
1/2 cup tamari
2 tablespoons toasted sesame oil
Zest from 1 lemon
1 tablespoon espelette pepper

30 sprigs thyme
1 bunch watercress

APRICOT MUSTARD CHUTNEY
6 ripe apricots
2 tablespoons yellow mustard seeds

1 tablespoon apple cider vinegar
1 tablespoon agave nectar
1/2 teaspoon sea salt

KING OYSTERS Cut mushrooms in half and score in a crosshatch design. Whisk the olive oil, vinegar, tamari, sesame oil, lemon zest, and pepper together in a large bowl. Toss the mushrooms in the dressing.

Place mushrooms in a vacuum bag with thyme. Vacuum seal bag at 100 percent and let marinate for at least 4 hours then cook the mushrooms in a sous vide water bath maintained at 115 degrees for 6 hours.

APRICOT MUSTARD CHUTNEY Dice apricots and place in a bowl. Add mustard seeds, vinegar, agave nectar, and salt; toss to combine. Seal in a jar and let set in refrigerator for 2 hours.

ASSEMBLY Remove mushrooms from sealed bag and pat dry with a paper towel. Reserve liquid.

Spoon 3 dollops of apricot mustard on each serving plate. Take a small handful of watercress and put on plates in between mustard dollops. Place 2 mushroom halves on top with the scored side facing up. Spoon reserved liquid over the mushrooms. Serve.

Portobello Salad

The cobb salad is a main-dish American garden salad made from chopped salad greens (iceberg lettuce, watercress, endives, and Romaine lettuce), tomato, crisp bacon, boiled or roasted (not fried) chicken breast, hard-boiled egg, avocado, and chives.

The cobb has seen so many twists and turns, but the spirit lives on in this version. What is most pleasurable about a cobb salad are the varied textures and it's simply just fun to eat. The smoked coconut bacon is awesome and addictive. —MK

6 cups mixed salad greens
2 avocados, peeled and sliced
1 cup sunflower sprouts

SOUS VIDE PORTOBELLOS
1/4 cup or more olive oil
Mixed chopped herbs (thyme, a bit of rosemary, tarragon, marjoram), to taste
1 scallion, chopped
1 tablespoon tamari
1 tablespoon sherry or balsamic vinegar
3 portobello tops, skinned and gilled

COCONUT BACON
1 teaspoon chipotle chile powder
1/2 cup maple syrup
1/4 cup cumin
1 cup filtered water
1 tablespoon olive oil
1 tablespoon tamari
1 tablespoon apple cider vinegar
1 teaspoon salt
1 tablespoon smoked paprika
2 cups coconut flakes

RED WINE VINAIGRETTE
1/4 cup red wine
1/4 cup rice vinegar
1 tablespoon lemon juice
1 tablespoon honey
1 teaspoon salt
1 cup olive oil

GARNISH
Edible flowers

SOUS VIDE PORTOBELLOS Whisk oil, herbs, scallion, tamari, and vinegar together in large bowl. Add portobellos and toss to coat. Remove portobellos from liquid but keep herbs and scallions; discard liquid.

Place mushrooms in a vacuum bag with herbs and scallions. Vacuum seal bag at 100 percent and let marinate for at least 4 hours then cook the mushrooms in a sous vide water bath maintained at 115 degrees for 6 hours.

continued

Portobello Salad ... continued

COCONUT BACON Blend chile powder, syrup, cumin, water, oil, tamari, vinegar, salt, and paprika in a blender until smooth. Combine with coconut flakes in a bowl and spread evenly in a thin layer on a nonstick dehydrator sheet. Dehydrate at 115 degrees for 8–10 hours, or until crispy throughout. Smoke the bacon with a smoking gun using apple wood. Place the bacon in a bowl, cover it with a lid or plastic wrap, and leave the smoking tube inside the bowl. Let smoke set covered in bowl for about 10 minutes.

RED WINE VINAIGRETTE Mix the wine, vinegar, lemon juice, honey, and salt in a blender. With the machine running, slowly blend in the oil.

ASSEMBLY Lightly toss salad greens in a large bowl with the Red Wine Vinaigrette. Divide salad greens among individual serving plates and then place avocado, Coconut Bacon, and portobellos around the salad. Top each serving with a large pinch of sunflower sprouts and a few flowers.

Endive. Lobster Mushroom.
GRAPEFRUIT. CUCUMBER. WAKAME.

Lobster "mushrooms" actually grow on mushrooms and their healthy mold is what gives them the lobster color. They even have a bit of a shellfish aroma when warmed. This is just a stunning dish. —MK

4 endives	2 tablespoons orange blossom	3 to 4 small lobster
2 white grapefruit	honey	mushrooms (about
1 tablespoon brown rice	1/2 teaspoon sea salt	1/4 pound)
vinegar	1/4 cup dry wakame	1 cup chervil leaves and stems
1/2 cup filtered water	1 large English cucumber	

Slice endives in half and place in a bowl. Supreme* grapefruit and reserve the juice. Set the sections aside in another bowl.

Make a dressing by whisking 1/2 cup reserved grapefruit juice, vinegar, water, honey, and salt together in a small bowl. Toss half of the dressing with the endives and set aside the other half.

Seal the endive pieces in a vacuum bag at 100 percent and refrigerate until ready to plate.

Rehydrate wakame by rinsing under cold filtered water and then let set covered with water until needed. Peel cucumber and slice into 1/4-inch rounds.

Strain wakame and toss with cucumber, grapefruit sections, and the rest of the dressing.

Thinly slice mushrooms horizontally using a mandolin, making sure the slices are thick enough to retain their shape.

ASSEMBLY Remove endives from sealed bag. Place 1 half on each serving plate and then cover the endive with 1/2 cup of wakame, cucumber, and grapefruit salad. Top the salad with sliced lobster mushrooms and chervil.

*To supreme a citrus fruit is when the skin is cut away from the fruit and the sections are cut out. Always cut the segments from the fruit over a bowl so you save the juice.

WHEN I REALLY CONSIDER WHAT I LOVE TO USE ON A DAILY BASIS, I note that many of my favorite ingredients are cured and preserved. What would we do without the olive! Curing, of course, serves many purposes from extending summer's bounty to intensifying flavor. Preserved lemons, delicious green olives, salty capers, and sweet, rich balsamic vinegars are all reminders of what we love about these foods. *—MK*

Cured

Cauliflower.
PRESERVED LEMON. WALNUT. HARISSA.

Some of our best dishes are created during the heat of the moment, on the fly in the restaurants, while others are developed in a more thoughtful way. Scott came to Maine during a beautiful summer week and rocked this out at Plantlab with produce from our favorite local market.

Harissa is a robust, often smoky hot sauce which originated in Tunisia. Like most hot sauces, this one has many variations, and of course, we have ours. It typically includes garlic, though keeping in fashion with our cuisine; we have left that ingredient out. It's one of those condiments that really is actually good with anything. —MK

WALNUT CREAM
1/2 cup walnuts, soaked overnight and peeled
1 cup filtered water
1 tablespoon walnut oil
Sea salt, to taste
6 sprigs thyme
1 (1- x 3-inch) piece kombu

CAULIFLOWER CRUMBLE
2 cups crumbled cauliflower
1/2 preserved lemon rind, finely minced
2 tablespoons walnut oil
Sea salt, to taste

SLICED CAULIFLOWER
1 small head white cauliflower
1 small head purple cauliflower
1 small head Romanesco
Walnut oil, to taste
Sea salt, to taste

HARISSA
1 cup olive oil
1 red bell pepper, seeded and deveined
2 tablespoons paprika
3 tablespoons lemon juice
2 tablespoons agave nectar
1 tablespoon red chile flakes
1 tablespoon cumin powder
1 tablespoon grated ginger
1/2 teaspoon coriander seeds
1 Thai bird chile pepper
1 teaspoon sea salt

SPICED WALNUTS
2 tablespoons tamari
1/2 cup maple syrup
1 tablespoon smoked paprika
1/2 teaspoon chili powder
1 cup walnuts

GARNISH
Micro watercress

Cauliflower ... continued

WALNUT CREAM Using a high-speed blender, blend walnuts, water, oil, and salt until very creamy. Place thyme and kombu in cream and let set for at least 1 hour to allow flavors to absorb.

CAULIFLOWER CRUMBLE Toss cauliflower and lemon with walnut oil and salt in a small bowl.

SLICED CAULIFLOWER Thinly slice the cauliflowers and toss with walnut oil and salt.

HARISSA Using a high-speed blender, thoroughly blend all ingredients and then strain through a chinois strainer at least 2 times.

SPICED WALNUTS Combine tamari, syrup, paprika, and chili powder in a small bowl. Add walnuts and stir to coat. Let walnuts marinate in mixture for at least an hour to absorb flavor. Place on dehydrator sheets and dehydrate at 115 degrees for 12 hours or until crispy.

ASSEMBLY In a shallow bowl using a 3-inch ring mold, fill mold with about $1/4$ cup Cauliflower Crumble. Spoon about 2 tablespoons of the Walnut Cream on top covering the crumble. Drop little dots of Harissa on top of cream. Take about 6 or 7 walnuts and stand them up in the crumble and cream mixture. Now take the Sliced Cauliflower and stand several pieces floret side down using the walnuts to help as a foundation. Garnish with micro watercress. Repeat process for all servings.

Cured Eggplant.
LEMON BALM. SHISITO PEPPER.

It's always a challenge to use eggplant raw. This dish was part of our opening tasting menu at M.A.K.E., and I think it is my favorite so far. —SW

There are a number of ways to create infusions, from the simplest method like this recipe, to making them in the Ultrasonic Homogenizer, which we have safely tucked away in Plantlab. These infusions are great to have in any active kitchen where a splash or a few drops of this or that can add depth to a very simply flavored dish. —MK

CURED EGGPLANT
1 medium Japanese eggplant
1 teaspoon sea salt, divided
1 1/2 cups apple cider vinegar
1 tablespoon red chile flakes
1/2 cup lemon juice
1 clove black garlic, minced
1/2 cup or more olive oil

SHISITO PEPPERS
2 cups shisito peppers, sliced
    into rounds
1 tablespoon olive oil
1 tablespoon lemon juice
Pinch of sea salt

LEMON BALM OIL
1 cup lemon balm, leaves only
1 tablespoon salt
1 cup grapeseed oil

GARNISH
Micro basil

CURED EGGPLANT Peel and slice the eggplant horizontally into very thin slices. Place the slices in a large bowl and toss with half the salt. Let set for 1 hour. Strain liquid and press the eggplant to remove additional liquid. Pat dry with a paper towel.

In a large bowl, mix vinegar, red chile flakes, lemon juice, garlic, remaining salt, and the oil to create a brine. Place eggplant in a canning jar and cover with brine. Store at room temperature for 72 hours to 4 weeks depending on how long you would like it to cure. The longer the eggplant cures, the more intense the flavor.

Cured eggplant will keep indefinitely, but once the jar is opened, it must be refrigerated.

continued

CURED

Cured Eggplant ... continued

SHISITO PEPPERS Toss peppers in oil, lemon juice, and salt.

LEMON BALM OIL Place lemon balm in a bowl, sprinkle with salt, and add the oil. Let steep for
10 minutes.

Using a high-speed blender, blend all ingredients together and then strain through a chinois strainer
2 times.

ASSEMBLY Remove cured eggplant from jar and place a large tablespoon of eggplant on each serving
plate. Top with 6 to 8 slices Shisito Peppers and about a teaspoon of Lemon Balm Oil per serving. Garnish
with micro basil.

Kelp Noodles.
BLACK PEPPER. CHANTERELLES.
SNAP PEAS. OLIVE. PEA TENDRILS.

SERVES 4–6

When Scott added this dish to our menu at M.A.K.E., in Santa Monica, it was an instant hit. While beautiful to look at, the flavors are bold and comfortable, reminiscent of the beloved Roman recipe, *Cacio e Pepe*, which translates to cheese and pepper.

The introduction of kelp noodles to the raw food arsenal of ingredients was a wonderful gift. These noodles, simply made from kelp, salt extracted from seaweed, and water, have little flavor, yet they are a textural wonder and also absorb the character of any sauce, particularly rich and bold ones. —MK

KELP NOODLES
1/2 bag kelp noodles
Warm water
1 teaspoon baking soda
1 teaspoon lemon juice
1/4 cup tamari
1 tablespoon olive oil
1 tablespoon agave nectar

BLACK PEPPER CREAM
1 cup cashews, soaked
    overnight

3/4 cup filtered water
1/2 tablespoon black
    peppercorns
1/4 cup lemon juice
1 tablespoon nutritional yeast
1 teaspoon sea salt

PEAS. BEANS. AND
CHANTERELLES
1 cup snap peas, deveined
1/2 cup yellow haricot jaune or
    wax beans

1/2 cup purple beans
1 cup chanterelle mushrooms
1 tablespoon lemon juice
1 tablespoon olive oil
Pinch of sea salt

CRISPY OLIVES
1 cup pitted whole black
    olives

GARNISH
Pea tendrils

KELP NOODLES Thoroughly rinse kelp noodles and place into a large bowl. Add water and baking soda and soak for 15 minutes. Rinse well.

continued

Kelp Noodles ... continued

Combine lemon juice, tamari, oil, and agave nectar and stir into noodles. Allow to marinate for at least 1 hour or as long as overnight. Using scissors, cut into small pieces before serving.

BLACK PEPPER CREAM Using a high-speed blender, blend all ingredients until smooth. Taste and adjust flavor, if needed.

PEAS. BEANS. AND CHANTERELLES Remove peas from the shells and set aside. Slice the pea shells, beans, and chanterelles and place in a bowl. Add the peas and toss with lemon juice, oil, and salt.

CRISPY OLIVES Place olives on dehydrator tray and dehydrate at 115 degrees for 8–12 hours or until crispy. Place dried olives in a food processor and pulse until olives become crumbly.

ASSEMBLY Toss Kelp Noodles with the Black Pepper Cream. Add Peas, Beans, and Chanterelles to the noodles and sauce and toss again.

Using about 1 cup per serving, place nicely in serving bowls. Garnish with a teaspoon of Crispy Olives sprinkled on top and a few pea tendrils stuck into the noodles so they stay standing.

Fennel Figs.
PISTACHIO. CALIFORNIA BALSAMIC.

A fresh, ripe fig in its prime season is a near perfect food. Despite it being known for sweetness, we prefer figs in savory compositions where they are balanced with non-sweet components and aromatics. Lemon, anise, and fig seem as natural a fit as tomato and basil. Black Mission figs are the fig of choice for this recipe, although green figs, when ripe, are also wonderful. —*MK*

I really like to use Bariani Balsamic Vinegar from California because it is sweet and has a nice tart bite. —*SW*

CURED FENNEL
4 fennel bulbs
1 cup olive oil
1/2 cup lemon juice
1 tablespoon sea salt
1/2 teaspoon black
   peppercorns

PISTACHIO-FENNEL PURÉE
1/2 cup pistachios, soaked
   overnight
1 tablespoon rice vinegar
1 tablespoon agave nectar
1 tablespoon fennel seeds
1/2 teaspoon salt
1/4 cup filtered water

FIGS
1 cup pistachios
Pinch of salt
Pinch of fennel pollen or
   ground fennel seeds
12 Black Mission figs
Balsamic vinegar

GARNISH
Fennel Flowers

CURED FENNEL Cut fennel into wedges. Mix oil, lemon juice, salt, and peppercorns to make a brine and then cover fennel with brine in a glass canning jar. Let set at room temperature out of direct sunlight for 7–12 days.

PISTACHIO-FENNEL PURÉE Place pistachios, vinegar, agave nectar, fennel seeds, and salt in a high-speed blender. Blend until creamy, adding filtered water, if needed, for desired texture. Pass through a strainer.

FIGS Using a microplane, make a dust of pistachios. Add salt and fennel pollen or ground fennel seeds and lightly mix; set aside. Slice figs in quarters and toss lightly in vinegar.

ASSEMBLY Place a tablespoon of Pistachio-Fennel Purée on each serving plate and lightly cover with pistachio-fennel dust. Top with a wedge of Cured Fennel. Place 3 fig slices next to fennel. Garnish with Fennel Flowers.

RAW CUISINE MAY NOT USE FIRE AND CLASSICAL REDUCTION METHODS, but we still find ways to intensify flavor and texture. Pressure is natural and preserves nutrients while still maximizing flavor and creating highly original dishes. These small dishes are also ideal for entertaining, as they hold up better than others if plated in advance, and a little goes a long way with the clean, but powerful flavors. —*MK*

Pressed

Walnut Terrine.
WATERMELON RADISH.
PICKLED CELERY. TOMATO WATER.

This is not a typical terrine made in a large mold and sliced to serve. We build it in individual molds. The flavors work really well together and the celery, radish, and tomato water cut through the fattiness of the walnuts. —*SW*

WALNUT TERRINE
1 cup walnuts, soaked
    overnight
1 tablespoon tamari
1 tablespoon olive oil
1 tablespoon parsley
1 teaspoon thyme leaves
1 teaspoon mushroom powder
Zest from half a lemon

PICKLED CELERY
1 tablespoon rice vinegar

1 teaspoon agave nectar
Pinch of salt
3 stalks celery, sliced
Pinch of red chile flakes

WATERMELON RADISH
1 medium watermelon radish

TOMATO WATER
1 pound vine-ripened red
    tomatoes (about 3 medium)

1/2 tablespoon coarse sea salt
2 (18- x 18-inch) pieces
    cheesecloth

GARNISH
Micro celery
Edible flowers

WALNUT TERRINE Using a food processor, pulse walnuts into small pieces. Place in a bowl and mix in tamari, oil, parsley, thyme, mushroom powder, and lemon zest.

PICKLED CELERY Whisk together vinegar, agave nectar, and salt in a bowl. Add the celery and chile flakes and toss. Remove the celery from the brine, place in a vacuum bag, and seal at 100 percent. The celery is now ready to serve. After opening the bag, store any leftovers in a sealable container.

WATERMELON RADISH Peel radish and thinly slice on a mandolin. Punch out circles using a small ring mold.

continued

PRESSED

103

Walnut Terrine ... continued

TOMATO WATER Rinse tomatoes under running water and cut in quarters. In a food processor, purée tomatoes with salt until smooth.

Line a strainer with both pieces cheesecloth and place over a tall nonreactive container. Pour tomato purée into cheesecloth. Gather sides of cheesecloth up over purée to form a large bag, and, without squeezing purée, gently gather together upper cheesecloth to form a neck. Carefully tie neck securely with kitchen string.

Tie bag to a wooden spoon that is longer than the diameter of the container and remove from strainer. Lay spoon across top of container with the bag hanging inside. Make sure to leave enough room so that the bag will not sit in the tomato water that accumulates. Refrigerate for at least 8 hours.

Without squeezing the bag, discard it and its contents, and transfer tomato water to a bowl. Tomato water keeps well covered and chilled for about 3 days.

ASSEMBLY Place a 1 1/2- x 3-inch rectangular mold in the bottom of a shallow bowl. Using a spoon, fill mold with walnut mixture and press down until it's about 1/3 filled and firm. Top with radish circles and celery in a shingle pattern. Garnish with micro celery and flowers. Remove mold. Repeat process for remainder of servings. Put Tomato Water in a small pitcher and pour into bowls tableside.

Compressed Melon.
BRAZIL NUT FETA. THAI BASIL.

I first tried this as an amuse and found it to be ideal as a palate cleanser and a vibrant wake-up call to the raw food I was about to experience. —*MK*

MELON
1 medium-size ripe honeydew melon, cut into 1-inch cubes
1 medium-size ripe cantaloupe, cut into 1-inch cubes

2 tablespoons lime juice
1 tablespoon olive oil
1 large pinch of sea salt

BRAZIL NUT FETA
2 cups Brazil nuts, soaked overnight

1/2 cup water
1 probiotic capsule
1 teaspoon sea salt

GARNISH
1 bunch Thai basil

MELON Toss melon cubes with lime juice, oil, and salt in a large bowl. Working with 12 cubes of melon at a time, place into a vacuum bag and seal at 100 percent. If using immediately, remove from vacuum bag, save liquid, pat dry with a paper towel, and serve.

BRAZIL NUT FETA Using a high-speed blender, blend all ingredients in a food processor. Transfer mixture into a chinois strainer lined with cheesecloth. Place chinois over a container to drain and tie up the ends of the cheesecloth to create a bundle for the cheese. Weigh down the bundle with something fairly heavy, like a jar of water. Culture at room temperature for at least 24 hours.

Press into molds and dehydrate at 115 degrees for 2 hours. The texture of the cheese will be crumbly.

ASSEMBLY Crumble Brazil Nut Feta and place some in the center of each serving plate. Reserving the liquid, remove melon cubes from the vacuum bags and pat dry. Place 5 to 7 pieces of melon around feta. Spoon reserved liquid over top and garnish with Thai basil leaves.

Compressed Apple.
CELERY. WALNUTS. MUSTARD SEEDS. FRISÉE.

This is my take on a dish that Chef Jason Paul created for one of our project nights. I am pretty sure Jason was going for the flavors of a Waldorf Salad. Sealing the apples with the celery juice is a nice touch and adds great flavor. —SW

COMPRESSED APPLES
1/2 cup celery juice*
1 tablespoon apple cider vinegar
1/2 teaspoon sea salt
4 Granny Smith apples, peeled

MUSTARD SEEDS
1 cup yellow mustard seeds

1/2 cup apple cider vinegar
1/4 cup water
1/4 cup agave nectar

SPICED WALNUTS
2 tablespoons tamari
1/2 cup maple syrup
1 tablespoon smoked paprika
1/2 teaspoon chili powder

1/2 cup walnuts

CELERY
2 stalks celery
2 cups ice water

GARNISH
Frisée

COMPRESSED APPLES Mix juice, vinegar, and salt in a bowl. Using a small melon baller, make as many apple balls as you can. Add apples to the juice mixture. Place in a vacuum bag and seal at 100 percent.

MUSTARD SEEDS Rinse mustard seeds with hot tap water. Combine vinegar, water, and agave nectar and toss with seeds. Place in a glass jar and let set, at room temperature, for at least 24 hours.

SPICED WALNUTS Combine tamari, syrup, paprika, and chili powder in a small bowl. Add walnuts and stir to coat. Let walnuts marinate in mixture for at least an hour to absorb flavor. Place on dehydrator sheets and dehydrate at 115 degrees for 12 hours or until crispy.

CELERY Using a vegetable peeler, peel strips of celery. Place in ice water to make crispy and curly celery.

ASSEMBLY Place a tablespoon of mustard seeds on the bottom of each serving plate or bowl. Remove apples from vacuum bag and place a few balls on top of mustard. Add a few walnuts and celery strips. Garnish with frisée.

Using an electric juicer, juice 4 stalks of celery for 1/2 cup celery juice.

Compressed Watermelon.
HERB PISTOU. NASTURTIUM

This dish is simple and delicious but still uses some modern techniques. The sweetness and the spiciness from the herbs and olive oil are a great refreshing blend with the sweet watermelon. —SW

WATERMELON
1 medium watermelon, seeded and sliced into 18 (2- x 4-inch) pieces

HERB PISTOU
1 cup nasturtium leaves and stems
1 cup basil leaves
1 cup tarragon leaves
$1/2$ teaspoon sea salt
$1/2$ cup olive oil

GARNISH
Flakey sea salt
Nasturtium leaves
Herbs, of choice

WATERMELON Working with 3 pieces of watermelon at a time, place into a vacuum bag and seal at 100 percent. When ready to serve, remove from vacuum bag and pat dry with a paper towel. The compressed watermelon is best used soon after sealing as the liquid tends to seep from melon and the fruit becomes less flavorful.

HERB PISTOU Using a food processor, process nasturtium, basil, tarragon, and salt until it is a purée. Slowly add the oil in while the processor is in motion. Try not to let your herb oil get too hot in the blender. Pass through a strainer.

ASSEMBLY Spoon 2 tablespoons of Herb Pistou on each serving plate. Place 3 slices of watermelon on top of pistou. Garnish with a sprinkle of flaky sea salt, nasturtium leaves, and herbs.

Mushroom Pâté.
APRICOTS. MUSTARD
HERB CRACKERS.

Without a doubt, this is the most elegant and refined raw food recipe I have tried. When Scott first prepared it, I wasn't expecting much as the ingredients don't really give a lot away, but one taste and anyone will be absolutely astonished. —*MK*

MUSHROOM PÂTÉ
3 cups chopped mushrooms
    (portobellos, oysters,
    shiitake)
1 cup walnuts
$1/2$ cup mushroom powder
1 tablespoon agave nectar
1 tablespoon tamari

1 tablespoon agar
1 teaspoon sesame oil

SPICED APRICOTS
1 cup sliced apricots
1 tablespoon apple cider
    vinegar
1 teaspoon grated ginger

1 teaspoon thyme leaves

MUSTARD HERB CRACKERS
1 cup flax seeds
$1/4$ cup yellow mustard
    powder
$1/2$ cup mixed herbs
$1/2$ cup water

MUSHROOM PÂTÉ Using a high-speed blender, blend all ingredients. (I use the soups/syrups setting on a Blendtec and run it 3 times.) The mixture must get hot to activate agar. Pour into a lined terrine mold and refrigerate for 2 hours to set.

SPICED APRICOTS Combine all ingredients together in a small bowl. Allow to marinate at least 1 hour before serving.

MUSTARD HERB CRACKERS Using a high-speed blender, blend all ingredients. Spread on teflex sheets, score into 2- x 3-inch rectangles, and dehydrate at 115 degrees for 12 hours or until dry and crisp.

ASSEMBLY Remove pâté from mold by carefully placing upside down on a large plate and lifting off mold form. Slice pâté into 1-inch-thick slices. Serve with crackers and apricots.

JUST A FEW SHORT YEARS AGO, we never would have guessed that fermented foods would be so hot. However, the shift in gourmet food, especially in contemporary restaurants such as Noma, in Copenhagen, coupled with more awareness of the benefits in healthy bacteria, has rapidly increased their use. Ferments are now one of the most exciting categories and one we embrace fully, both for their nutritional benefits and for their depth and uniqueness of flavor. —MK

Fermented

Summer Squash.
SAFFRON YOGURT. BLACK OLIVE.

This dish is best at the peak of summer. Using a variety of squash makes an excellent salad. —*SW*

SUMMER SQUASH
2 medium zucchini
2 medium goldbar squash
4 small pattypan squash
12 sungold or heirloom cherry
    tomatoes
Pinch of sea salt

SAFFRON YOGURT
2 cups cashews, soaked
    overnight
1 probiotic capsule
1 tablespoon apple cider vinegar

Sea salt, to taste
A heavy pinch of saffron

BLACK OLIVE OIL
1 cup pitted whole black olives
1/2 cup olive oil
1/2 cup water

THYME OIL
1 cup fresh thyme leaves
1 teaspoon salt
2 cups olive oil

SHERRY THYME DRESSING
1 cup sherry vinegar
1 tablespoon ras el hanout
    powder
1 teaspoon salt
1/2 teaspoon chile flakes
1 cup Thyme Oil
1 cup olive oil

GARNISH
6 zucchini or squash blossoms
1/2 cup fresh mint leaves

SUMMER SQUASH Cut and slice squash into various shapes. Slice tomatoes in half.

SAFFRON YOGURT Using a high-speed blender, blend cashews and probiotic capsule to a yogurt-like consistency, adding a little water, if needed. Cover and let set for 8–12 hours. Place yogurt in blender and add vinegar and salt; blend. Rub saffron threads between fingers as you let it fall into mixture in blender. Stir lightly with a spoon and let bloom in yogurt for 5 minutes. Blend until creamy.

BLACK OLIVE OIL Using a high-speed blender, blend all ingredients together. Pass through a strainer.

THYME OIL Steep thyme and salt in oil, at room temperature, for 12–24 hours. Blend all ingredients together and strain through a chinois strainer at least 2 times.

SHERRY THYME DRESSING Blend vinegar, ras el hanout, salt, and chile flakes together. With the blender running, slowly pour in oils to emulsify.

ASSEMBLY Place squash and tomatoes in a bowl and toss with the dressing and a pinch of sea salt. Put a healthy dollop of Saffron Yogurt off center on each serving plate. Using a small offset spatula, spread the yogurt across the plate making a bed for the salad. Build salads using all different shapes and varieties of the squash and the tomatoes. Drop some dots of Black Olive Oil on the salads using a squeeze bottle. Garnish each plate with a squash blossom and mint leaves.

Pickled Plum.
SHISO. HORSERADISH CRISP.

Japanese chefs are masters at the art of pickling and employing bursts of briny flavor throughout a meal, much in the way a great musician will implement a variety of tones to keep the flow going. This style is definitely tart, yet equalized with sweetness, so the overall effect is powerful while still not overwhelming. —*MK*

PLUMS
1/4 cup rice vinegar
1 tablespoon agave nectar
1 tablespoon minced ginger
1/4 teaspoon sea salt
6 unripe plums

SHISO CREAM
1 cup almonds, soaked
  overnight

1/2 cup filtered water
1/2 cup fresh shiso leaves
1 tablespoon pickled plum
  brine
1/2 teaspoon sea salt

HORSERADISH CRISPS
1 cup flax seeds
1 cup peeled and chopped
  horseradish

1/2 cup water
1 teaspoon salt

GARNISH
Micro shiso

PLUMS Mix vinegar, agave nectar, ginger, and salt in a bowl to make a brine. Slice plums in half and remove the pits. Add plums to brine and toss to combine. Let plums set in brine for at least 2 hours at room temperature. Strain from brine and seal in a vacuum bag at 100 percent. Refrigerate.

SHISO CREAM Using a high-speed blender, blend all ingredients until completely smooth, adding more water, if needed, to reach desired consistency. Pass through a strainer to remove any clumps.

HORSERADISH CRISPS Using a high-speed blender, blend all ingredients until thoroughly combined. Spread on a teflex sheet. Dehydrate at 115 degrees for 8 hours or until crisp. Hand break into rough shapes.

ASSEMBLY Slice plums into wedges, and place randomly on individual serving plates. Using a squeeze bottle, put Shiso Cream dollops around and close to plums. Place Horseradish Crisps so they are sticking up lying against the plums. Garnish with micro shiso.

Kimchee Dumplings.

While having a vegan tasting menu at the bar of one of Boston's best restaurants, O-Ya, I was served a kimchee dumpling, made with a fresh, thin dough, rich and garlicky, and full of flavor. I liked it a lot, but I liked the idea of it even more. We set about making our own raw version a few years ago. This has since become one of our signature dishes and likely the most photographed. —MK

PURPLE KIMCHEE
1 head purple cabbage
4 tablespoons sea salt, divided
1 quart cold water
1 tablespoon minced garlic
1 tablespoon minced ginger
1 teaspoon red chile flakes

KIMCHEE FILLING
1 cup raw cashews, soaked
 overnight
1/2 tablespoon tamari
1/2 tablespoon sesame oil
1 tablespoon raw tahini
1 teaspoon agave nectar
1/2 cup Purple Kimchee

CILANTRO WRAPPERS
2 cups young coconut meat
1/4 teaspoon sea salt
1/4 cup cilantro-spinach juice*

SESAME GINGER FOAM
1/2 cup ginger juice**
1/4 cup sesame oil
1 teaspoon agave nectar
1/2 teaspoon lecithin

KIMCHEE PURÉE
1 cup Purple Kimchee
1/2 cup Purple Kimchee brine
1/4 cup olive oil

GARNISH
Micro cilantro
Edible flowers

PURPLE KIMCHEE Day 1: Separate and wash cabbage leaves. Dilute 3 tablespoons of salt in the water. Place cabbage leaves in the water, being sure that the water completely covers all the leaves. Put a plate or other heavy object on top of leaves to ensure that they stay submerged. Refrigerate overnight.

Day 2: Pour off water and thoroughly rinse cabbage leaves. Shake them gently in the sink to remove excess moisture.

Make a paste out of the garlic, ginger, red chile flakes, and remaining salt. Tear cabbage leaves into a large bowl and add paste. Use your hands to rub paste evenly onto all cabbage leaves. Transfer seasoned cabbage leaves into a large glass jar. Be sure to use firm pressure with your hands to push down on the cabbage as it is packed inside the jar. Transfer any liquid that accumulated during the mixing process into the bottle as well.

FERMENTED

continued

117

Kimchee Dumplings ... continued

This liquid will become kimchee brine. Some liquid will also come out of the cabbage leaves as you press down on them as they are stacked in the jar. Leave about 2 inches of room at the top of the jar before capping it tightly with a lid. Allow kimchee to set at room temperature for 2–3 days.

KIMCHEE FILLING Process cashews, tamari, oil, tahini, agave nectar, and kimchee in a food processor until a chunky consistency is achieved. If the mixture is wet, press out the excess liquid through a chinois strainer.

CILANTRO WRAPPERS Using a high-speed blender, blend coconut, salt, and juice until very smooth. Spread mixture in a thin, even layer over 2 teflex sheets. Dehydrate for 4–5 hours at 115 degrees. Once dry but still pliable, remove from dehydrator and gently peel off teflex sheets. Cut wrappers into 18 (3 1/2-inch) squares. Store on tray with parchment paper between layers, sealing the whole tray tightly with plastic wrap.

SESAME GINGER FOAM Combine all ingredients in a blender.

KIMCHEE PURÉE Place kimchee and brine in a high-speed blender and blend to combine. Add oil at slow setting to make the purée. Pass through a strainer.

ASSEMBLY Using a spoon or squeeze bottle, drizzle individual serving plates with the Kimchee Purée.

Place a tablespoon of the Kimchee Filling in the middle of each Cilantro Wrapper. Bring corners to the middle and press together to make the dumplings. Place 3 dumplings on each plate on top of the purée.

Using an immersion blender, foam up the Sesame Ginger Foam and spoon about a teaspoon on top of each dumpling. Garnish with micro cilantro and some edible flowers.

Using a electric juicer, juice a handful of spinach and cilantro. The spinach will keep the cilantro from oxidizing. Strain juice.

Using an electric juicer, juice peeled ginger. Strain juice.

Heirloom Carrot.
CASHEW YOGURT. CUMIN CRISP.

SERVES 4

This recipe was one of the first signature dishes at M.A.K.E., and an early example of our new, cleaner style of raw food that we have come to embrace. —*MK*

RAINBOW CARROTS
12 small rainbow heirloom
    carrots
Pinch of sea salt
1 tablespoon apple cider
    vinegar
1 tablespoon olive oil

CASHEW YOGURT
2 cups cashews, soaked
    overnight

1 probiotic capsule
1 tablespoon apple cider
    vinegar
1/2 teaspoon cumin
Sea salt, to taste

CARROT CUMIN CRISPS
2 large carrots
1 tablespoon cumin seeds
1/2 cup water

1 tablespoons agave nectar
1/2 teaspoon salt
1/2 teaspoon berbere spice*

GARNISH
1/2 cup carrot tops or flat-leaf
    parsley leaves

RAINBOW CARROTS Slice carrots vertically and very thin using a mandolin. Place in a bowl and add salt, vinegar, and oil. Toss to combine and marinate for a few minutes until carrots are well flavored.

CASHEW YOGURT Using a high-speed blender, blend cashews and probiotic capsule to a yogurt-like consistency, adding a little water, if needed. Cover and let set for 8–12 hours, or overnight.

Place yogurt in a blender and blend with vinegar, cumin and salt.

CARROT CUMIN CRISPS Using a high-speed blender, blend all ingredients until smooth. Thinly spread on teflex sheets and dehydrate at 115 degrees for 12 hours or until completely dry. Break apart into rough-shaped crisps.

ASSEMBLY Spread about 2 tablespoons Cashew Yogurt on the bottom of shallow bowls for each serving. Place some carrots on top of yogurt, building a tight ball, and add a few Carrot Cumin Crisps. Garnish with carrot leaves or parsley.

Berbere spice is a spice blend native to Ethiopia. Like curries in India, Ethiopian families often have their own blend of this spice. The blend usually consists of chiles, garlic, ginger, and dried basil.

ONE OF THE THINGS THAT REALLY TURNED MY HEAD WHEN I first started becoming familiar with raw foods was cheeses made from different nuts. We are continually expanding our recipes and learning how to make them better in all ways from taste, to texture, and to color.

The evolution of raw tree nut cheese is certainly a high point of my experience with plant-based cuisine. We have a cheese tasting class in our Fundamentals of Raw Cuisine course—the third Friday of every month. I never forget that day! These are just incredible, deep flavored, and loved by all. The versatility of the flavoring is one of the best aspects, in that the fermentation process really sets the groundwork for a multitude of opportunities. I'm partial to earthy flavors, porcini, truffle, or just plain, but it's also fun to play, as we've done in this chapter, and as you should too. —MK

I would like to thank Sean Murray, our lead instructor at Matthew Kenney Culinary in Santa Monica for his knowledge and experience in developing our tree nut cheeses. He answered a lot of questions in this chapter and every time we make a new batch at M.A.K.E. I am sure to have a few more inquiries about what Sean has going on with his path to tree nut cheese perfection. —SW

Aged

Tree Nut Cheeses.
MARKET FRUIT. SWEET AND SPICY MUSTARD SEEDS. FENNEL CRISPS.

Matthew and I actually met over a mustard conversation. He asked me what my favorite food was—and I said mustard. At the time, I had just returned from abroad in France and I absolutely fell in love with the Dijon there. This particular recipe is a stone-ground version—the flavor is every bit as good, and the texture is a necessary addition to a cheese board. —MB

FENNEL CRISPS
2 cups almond flour
1/4 cup olive oil
2 cups peeled and roughly
   chopped zucchini
1 tablespoon lemon juice
1 tablespoon nutritional yeast
1/2 tablespoon salt
1/2 cup flax meal
2 tablespoons fennel seeds

MUSTARD
1/2 cup brown mustard seeds
1/2 cup yellow mustard seeds
1/4 cup yellow mustard
   powder
1/2 cup apple cider vinegar
1/2 cup agave nectar
1/2 cup water
1 tablespoon sea salt

PICKLED SEASONAL FRUIT
1 cup sliced fruit (apples,
   pears, berries, stone fruit)
1 tablespoon apple cider
   vinegar
1 teaspoon grated ginger
1 teaspoon thyme leaves

FENNEL CRISPS Using a high-speed blender, blend flour, oil, zucchini, lemon juice, nutritional yeast, and salt until smooth. Pour contents of blender into a bowl, add flax meal and fennel seeds, and mix by hand.

Allow to set for 2–5 minutes then spread batter approximately 1/4 inch thick onto a teflex sheet. Dehydrate at 115 degrees for 1 hour then score into 1 1/2- x 3-inch rectangles. Return to dehydrator for 12 hours or until completely dry.

MUSTARD Mix all ingredients together in a bowl. Let set for about an hour to allow the mustard seeds to bloom. Remove half of the mixture and blend in a high-speed blender then pour back into the remaining mixture. Stir. You may need to adjust the amount of liquid and/or agave nectar to achieve the desired consistency and sweetness. Let set out at room temperature for 1–2 days then refrigerate.

PICKLED SEASONAL FRUIT Combine fruit, vinegar, ginger and thyme and store in a glass jar until serving.

ASSEMBLY Serve an assortment of the following cheese recipes with Fennel Crisps, Mustard, and Pickled Seasonal Fruit on the side.

SIMPLE NUT CHEESE

| 2 cups macadamias or cashews, soaked overnight | 1/2 cup water (just enough to blend thoroughly—may need more for macadamia nuts or less for cashews) | 1 probiotic capsule
1/4 teaspoon sea salt
1 teaspoon nutritional yeast
1/2 teaspoon lemon juice |

Blend nuts, water, and probiotic capsule in a high-speed blender until smooth. Transfer mixture into a strainer lined with cheesecloth. Set strainer over a container to drain and tie up the ends of the cheesecloth to create a bundle for the cheese. Weigh down the bundle with something slightly heavy, like a jar of water. Strainer needs to be placed in a bowl or vessel that prevents the cheese from sitting in its own liquid. Ferment at room temperature for at least 24 hours.

After 24 hours, smell the cheese. It should have a slightly sour, fermented smell. If it just smells like soaked nuts, it has not fermented enough. If it is ready, split open the cheese in half (like breaking a roll). The inside should look spongy. These are air pockets caused by the release of CO_2 by microorganisms, typically lactobacillus, during the fermentation process. Once fermentation is complete, stir in or use a food processor to mix in salt, nutritional yeast, and lemon juice.

Press the cheese into a ring mold. Fill the mold not quite to the top, using the back of a spoon to press down and spread the cheese base flat into the mold. Allow to set up in the mold for at least 48 hours in a refrigerator, or 6 hours in a freezer before removing cheese from the mold.

IF YOU USED MACADAMIAS: At this point you can remove the ring mold and place in the refrigerator or remove the ring mold and place in a dehydrator at 115 degrees for 12–36 hours to get a rind.

IF YOU USED CASHEWS: At this point you can either place in the refrigerator, still in the ring mold as it's not as firm as macadamia cheese, for 24 hours and then remove the mold. Or you can place in the freezer to set harder for 1–2 hours and then remove the ring mold and place the whole thing in the dehydrator for 24 hours at 115 degrees to get a rind.

SMOKED CASHEW CHEDDAR CHEESE

2 cups cashews, soaked
   overnight
1/4 cup red bell pepper juice*

1/4 cup water
1 probiotic capsule
1 tablespoon nutritional yeast

3/4 teaspoon salt
1 tablespoon lemon juice
Pinch of turmeric

Blend cashews, pepper juice, water, and probiotic capsule in a high-speed blender until smooth. Transfer mixture into a strainer lined with cheesecloth. Set the strainer over a container to drain and tie up the ends of the cheesecloth to create a bundle for the cheese. Weigh down the bundle with something slightly heavy, like a jar of water. Ferment at room temperature for at least 24 hours.

After 24 hours, smell the cheese. It should have a slightly sour, fermented smell. If it just smells like soaked nuts, it has not fermented enough. If it is ready, split open the cheese in half (like breaking a roll). The inside should look spongy. These are air pockets caused by the release of CO_2 by microorganisms, typically lactobacillus, during the fermentation process. Once fermentation is complete, stir in or use a food processor to mix in nutritional yeast, salt, lemon juice, and turmeric.

Place cheese into a wide-bottom pan or bowl. Cover with plastic wrap and smoke cheese with a smoking gun using a mix of hickory and apple wood. This cheese should be smoked twice. After flavor components have been thoroughly mixed, smoked, and let set until smoke has been absorbed for 15–20 minutes, stir in smoked top layer of cheese then spread flat and smoke again. Thoroughly mix again once second round of smoking has been absorbed.

Press the cheese into a ring mold. Fill the mold not quite to the top, using the back of a spoon to press down and spread the cheese base flat into the mold. Allow to set up in the mold for at least 48 hours in a refrigerator, or 6 hours in a freezer before removing cheese from the mold. Dehydrate cheese at 115 degrees for 8–12 hours to create a rind.

Using an electric juicer, juice 1 seeded red bell pepper for 1/4 cup juice.

TRUFFLE MACADAMIA CHEESE

2 cups macadamia nuts,	1 probiotic capsule	1 tablespoon truffle oil
soaked overnight	1 tablespoon nutritional yeast	
1/2 cup water	3/4 teaspoon salt	

Blend nuts, water, and probiotic capsule in a high-speed blender until smooth. Transfer mixture into a strainer lined with cheesecloth. Set strainer over a container to drain and tie up the ends of the cheesecloth to create a bundle for the cheese. Weigh down the bundle with something slightly heavy, like a jar of water. Ferment at room temperature for at least 24 hours.

After 24 hours, smell the cheese. It should have a slightly sour, fermented smell. If it just smells like soaked nuts, it has not fermented enough. If it is ready, split open the cheese in half (like breaking a roll). The inside should look spongy. These are air pockets caused by the release of CO_2 by microorganisms, typically lactobacillus, during the fermentation process. Once fermentation is complete, stir in or use a food processor to mix in nutritional yeast, salt, and truffle oil.

Press the cheese into a ring mold. Fill the mold not quite to the top, using the back of a spoon to press down and spread the cheese base flat into the mold. Allow to set up in the mold for at least 48 hours in a refrigerator, or 6 hours in a freezer before removing cheese from mold. Dehydrate cheese at 115 degrees for 8–12 hours to create a rind.

HERBED CHÈVRE-STYLE CHEESE

2 cups cashews, soaked	1 teaspoon salt	1 teaspoon minced dill
overnight	2 tablespoons nutritional yeast	2 teaspoons thyme leaves
1/2 cups water	1 teaspoon lemon juice	1 teaspoon minced flat-leaf
1 probiotic capsule	Zest from 1 lemon	parsley

Blend nuts, water, and probiotic capsule in a high-speed blender until smooth. Transfer mixture into a strainer lined with cheesecloth. Set strainer over a container to drain and tie up the ends of the cheesecloth to create a bundle for the cheese. Weigh down the bundle with something slightly heavy, like a jar of water. Ferment at room temperature for no more than 24 hours.

After 24 hours, smell the cheese. It should have a slightly sour fermented smell. If it just smells like soaked nuts, it has not fermented enough. If it is ready, split open the cheese in half (like breaking a roll). The inside should look spongy. These are air pockets caused by the release of CO_2 by microorganisms, typically lactobacillus, during the fermentation process. Once fermentation is complete, stir in or use a food processor to mix in salt, nutritional yeast, lemon juice, and zest. Blend until well incorporated.

To shape the cheese, transfer to a sheet of parchment paper and evenly roll to form a log. Once tightly rolled, let age in refrigerator for 2–3 days. Once the cheese has firmed up a bit, spread herbs out over a 10- x 18-inch sheet of parchment paper. Remove the aged cheese from its parchment, place on top of herbs on the new parchment paper, roll, and evenly coat in the herbs. Once thoroughly coated, roll in new parchment, and let set in refrigerator until ready to serve. Refrigerate for up to 10 days.

SPIRULINA BLUE CHEESE

2 cups cashews, soaked overnight	1 probiotic capsule	1 teaspoon lemon juice
$1/2$ cup water	2 teaspoons nutritional yeast	Pinch of spirulina
	$3/4$ teaspoon salt	

Blend nuts, water, and probiotic capsule in a high-speed blender until smooth. Transfer mixture into a strainer lined with cheesecloth. Set strainer over a container to drain and tie up the ends of the cheesecloth to create a bundle for the cheese. Weigh down the bundle with something slightly heavy, like a jar of water. Ferment at room temperature for at least than 24 hours.

After 24 hours, smell the cheese. It should have a slightly sour, fermented smell. If it just smells like soaked nuts, it has not fermented enough. If it is ready, split open the cheese in half (like breaking a roll). The inside should look spongy. These are air pockets caused by the release of CO_2 by microorganisms, typically lactobacillus, during the fermentation process. Once fermentation is complete, stir in or use a food processor to mix in nutritional yeast, salt, and lemon juice to thoroughly combine.

Fold in spirulina to make cheese look marbled. To do this, spread cheese $1/4$ inch thick on the bottom of a sheet pan. Sprinkle a little of the spirulina into a 3–4-inch line. Gently fold the cheese over the line of spirulina so that the spirulina is covered by the cheese, but not mixed with the cheese. Repeat this process until desired marbling has been reached or spirulina has been all used.

To shape the cheese, transfer to a 10- x 18-inch sheet of parchment paper and evenly roll to form a log. Once tightly rolled, let age in refrigerator for 2–3 days until serving. Refrigerate for up to 10 days.

DESSERTS ARE ONE OF THE MOST SPECIAL PARTS OF RAW FOODS—the most "impressive" if you will. When you present someone with a beautifully plated, decadent, and delicious dessert, the reaction is often an expression of awe. How could this be so amazing without using dairy, eggs, or refined sweeteners?

Most of us are conditioned to think that desserts aren't healthy. We pride ourselves on challenging that theory. Never could I have imagined how evolved our recipes would become. When I first started in raw food—all of the desserts were nut heavy and bulky. Tasty, but definitely not refined. Over the years our evolution has been pretty remarkable. Part of this process is owed to the talented pastry wizards that we've had in our kitchens over the years, most notably Tatiana Jankowski. Tatiana's approach to dessert is full of whimsy and delight. Every flavor and combination is a surprise. This chapter features many recipes that were inspired by her, and represent her influence in our pastry department.

We have used agave nectar in many of these recipes because the flavor is neutral. The key with using agave is finding a very high quality organic agave. There are many on the market that are poor quality and mass produced. If you aren't comfortable using agave, use your preferred liquid sweetener of choice—coconut nectar, honey, and maple syrup all make interesting substitutions. —*MB*

Sweetened

Chocolate Cake. Walnut.
LICORICE. PEAR. FENNEL. SASSAFRAS.

This dish was one of our best selling desserts on our opening menu at M.A.K.E. The base of this cake is like a dense, flourless chocolate brownie. The additional spices and fruit cut through some of the heavy chocolate flavor to cleanse the palate and keep the flavor fresh. If you don't have time to make all of the components, the cake is great served with something simple like vanilla ice cream or just the Walnut Caramel. —*MB*

CINNAMON CHOCOLATE CAKE

DRY
1 cup oat flour
2 tablespoons ground
    flax seeds
1 cup hazelnut pulp*
2 1/2 cups almonds, finely
    ground into flour
1/3 cup cacao powder
1 teaspoon vanilla
1 teaspoon cinnamon

WET
1/2 cup Irish moss paste**
1/3 cup hazelnut milk
    (page 146)
1/2 cup pecans
1/2 cup walnuts
1/3 cup dates
1/3 cup coconut oil
1 tablespoon agave nectar
1 cup maple syrup
1 cup cacao paste

1 cup cacao powder

WALNUT CARAMEL
1/4 cup walnuts
1/4 cup maple syrup
1 tablespoon walnut oil
1/4 cup filtered water
2 dates
1/4 teaspoon lecithin
Pinch of salt
1 tablespoon coconut oil

FENNEL GEL
1 small fennel bulb, juiced
1 tablespoon agave nectar
1/2 teaspoon lemon juice
1 tablespoon coconut oil
1/4 teaspoon xanthan gum
Pinch of salt

ANISE COMPRESSED PEARS
1 pear, thinly sliced
3/4 tablespoon apple cider
    vinegar
1/2 tablespoon lemon juice
3 tablespoons water
1 1/2 tablespoons Pernod
1/8 teaspoon anise extract
1 tablespoon agave nectar
Pinch of salt

SASSAFRAS TEA
1/4 cup dried sassafras bark
1 cup hot water
1/2 cup agave nectar

SASSAFRAS ICE CREAM
1/2 cup cashews, soaked
    overnight
1/2 cup coconut meat
1/2 cup sassafras tea
1 tablespoon maple syrup
1 teaspoon vanilla extract
1/4 teaspoon vanilla bean
    powder
2 licorice drops
1/8 teaspoon salt
1/2 tablespoon cacao butter,
    melted
1 tablespoon coconut oil,
    melted

CANDIED FENNEL SEEDS
1/2 cup fennel seeds
3 tablespoons maple syrup
1 tablespoon water
Pinch of salt

continued

CINNAMON CHOCOLATE CAKE Place all of the dry ingredients into a large bowl and set aside. Add all the wet ingredients, except for cacao paste, to high-speed blender and blend until smooth. Add the blender contents to the dry ingredients. Melt the cacao paste over warm water then add to the bowl. Mix everything together by hand.

Portion cake batter into 12 ($1/3$-cup) balls, roll in cacao powder and press into $2 1/2$-inch ring molds. Dehydrate cakes on teflex sheets at 115 degrees overnight.

WALNUT CARAMEL Using a high-speed blender, blend all ingredients, except for the coconut oil, until perfectly smooth. Add oil last and continue to blend until well incorporated. Place in a squeeze bottle or store in a sealable container.

FENNEL GEL Blend all of the ingredients until smooth. Store in a squeeze bottle.

ANISE COMPRESSED PEARS Using a mandolin, thinly slice pears, horizontally, into circles. Combine vinegar, lemon juice, water, Pernod, anise extract, agave nectar, and salt in a bowl and toss with pear slices. Layer sliced pears in a vacuum bag. Pour a few tablespoons of the extra liquid into the bag and seal at 100 percent.

SASSAFRAS TEA Steep sassafras bark in hot water for 15–30 minutes then, using a high-speed blender, blend tea, bark, and agave nectar until finely broken down. Strain through a fine chinois strainer, discard pulp, and reserve sweet tea to make ice cream.

SASSAFRAS ICE CREAM Using a high speed blender, blend all ingredients except for cacao butter and coconut oil, until perfectly smooth. Add butter and oil, and continue to blend until everything is well incorporated. Place in a Pacojet canister or a quart container and freeze following the manufacturer's instructions. You can also use a standard ice cream machine.

CANDIED FENNEL SEEDS Toss all ingredients together and spread on a teflex sheet. Dehydrate at 115 degrees for at least 24 hours or until dry.

ASSEMBLY Spread a few drops each of the Fennel Gel and the Walnut Caramel on each serving plate.

Remove cakes from dehydrator. Push an indentation in each cake with your thumb and squeeze about a tablespoon of caramel into each one. Place cakes off center on the plates. Remove pear from the vacuum bag and place 1 or 2 slices rolled up by each cake. Make a quenelle shapes from the ice cream and put one next to the cakes. Sprinkle with Candied Fennel Seeds.

*Hazelnut pulp is leftover when you make hazelnut milk. See page 146.

**Irish moss paste is made by blending 2 cups soaked and thoroughly rinsed Irish moss, $1/2$ cup water, and $1/4$ cup lemon juice until smooth. You may need to add more water to achieve a smooth consistency. The mixture should not be watery or chunky. This will make approximately 3 cups and will keep up to 2 weeks stored in the refrigerator.

Maca Sorbet.
CARAMELIZED CACAO. SALTED MAPLE ALMONDS.

Malted chocolate goodness is the best way to describe this dish. Although maca is a superfood supplement, the flavor lends itself well to all things creamy and chocolatey. —*MB*

ALMOND MACA SORBET
1 cup almonds
2 cups water
1/2 cup cashews
1/4 cup maple syrup
1/2 cup maca powder

CARAMELIZED CACAO
1/2 cup raw cacao nibs
1/4 cup maple syrup
Pinch of sea salt

SALTED MAPLE ALMONDS
2 cups almonds
1/2 cup maple syrup
1 teaspoon sea salt

ALMOND MACA SORBET Using a high-speed blender, blend almonds and water thoroughly. Strain and remove almond pulp. Blend remaining cream with cashews, syrup, and maca powder. Use preferred ice cream machine to make sorbet.

CARAMELIZED CACAO Mix cacao, syrup, and salt in a bowl. Spread all ingredients on a teflex sheet and dehydrate at 115 degrees for 8 hours or until dry.

SALTED MAPLE ALMONDS Toss all ingredients in a bowl, spread on a teflex sheet and dehydrate at 115 degrees overnight or until completely dry. Using a chef's knife, roughly chop.

ASSEMBLY Place 2 scoops of sorbet in each serving bowl and top with a tablespoon of Caramelized Cacao and a tablespoon of almonds. Serve.

Apple Pie. Rosemary.
CRANBERRY. CREAM CHEESE SORBET.

This is our modern take on a baked apple pie. The flavor is every bit as good as the traditional pie and is enhanced by the flavors of cranberry, rosemary, and cream cheese. This is one of my personal favorites. —MB

CRANBERRY SPLASH
1 cup cranberries, fresh or frozen and thawed
1 1/2 tablespoons agave nectar
1 1/2 tablespoons maple syrup
1 teaspoon lemon juice
Pinch of salt
1/8 teaspoon xanthan gum

CREAM CHEESE SORBET
1/2 cup cashews, soaked overnight
3/4 cup coconut meat
1/2 cup cashew milk (page 146)
1/2 cup water
1/4 cup flax gel*
2 tablespoons lemon juice
1/2 teaspoon lemon extract
1/2 lemon, zested
2 tablespoons honey
2 tablespoons maple syrup
1/2 tablespoon agave nectar
1/4 teaspoon nutritional yeast
Pinch of sea salt
1 tablespoon coconut oil

ROSEMARY MILK SORBET
1/4 cup cashews, soaked overnight
1/4 cup loosely packed rosemary leaves
1/2 cup coconut meat
1/2 cup cashew milk (page 146)
1/2 tablespoon agave nectar
1/2 teaspoon lemon juice
Pinch of salt
1/2 tablespoon coconut oil, melted
A few pinches of spirulina

BAKED APPLES
12 small apples, peeled
1/2 cup apple juice
1/4 cup lemon juice
2 teaspoons cinnamon
1/4 teaspoon ground nutmeg (grind using a microplane)
1/4 teaspoon ginger powder
1/3 cup agave nectar
1/3 cup coconut sugar
1/4 teaspoon salt

APPLE GEL
1 cup apple juice
1/4 teaspoon xanthan gum

SPICED DRIED APPLES
2 small Granny Smith apples
1 1/2 tablespoons maple syrup
1/2 teaspoon lemon juice
Pinch of salt
1/2 teaspoon apple pie spice

ROSEMARY OLIVE OIL CRUST AND CRUMBLE

DRY
1/4 cup coconut flour
1/4 cup oat flour
1/4 teaspoon vanilla powder
1 tablespoon maple powder
1/8 teaspoon salt
1 teaspoon nutritional yeast
1/4 cup flax seeds, ground
1/2 cup cashews
1/2 cup hazelnuts
1/2 cup macadamia nuts

WET
2 tablespoons fresh rosemary leaves
1/4 cup olive oil
1 tablespoon agave nectar
1/4 teaspoon salt
1/2 tablespoon cacao butter, melted

CRANBERRY SPLASH Blend the cranberries, agave nectar, and syrup until perfectly smooth; strain through a fine chinois strainer. Then blend the strained purée with the lemon juice, salt, and xanthan gum. Store in a sealable container.

CREAM CHEESE SORBET Using a high-speed blender, blend all ingredients, except for the coconut oil, until perfectly smooth. Add the oil and continue to blend until everything is well incorporated.

Store in quart containers and freeze. To make disks, defrost, re-blend until smooth, pour into a squeeze bottle and squeeze out 1 1/4-inch disks onto parchment paper. Freeze to set and store, frozen, in a flat sealable container.

ROSEMARY MILK SORBET Using a high-speed blender, blend all ingredients, except for the coconut oil and spirulina, until perfectly smooth. Add the oil and spirulina and continue to blend until everything is well incorporated.

Store in quart containers and freeze. To make disks, defrost, re-blend until smooth, pour into a squeeze bottle and squeeze out 1 1/4-inch disks onto parchment paper. Freeze to set and store, frozen, in a flat sealable container.

BAKED APPLES Peel and core apples and thinly slice using a mandolin. Combine apple juice, lemon juice, cinnamon, nutmeg, ginger powder, agave nectar, sugar, and salt into a large bowl. Toss apple slices in mixture and place on a flat, wide pan. Dehydrate overnight at 115 degrees or until the apples are tender. Strain the apples in the morning and store in sealable containers. Use the strained juice to make the Apple Gel.

APPLE GEL Dehydrate juice at 115 degrees until it becomes slightly concentrated, approximately 24 hours. Blend dehydrated juice and xanthan gum until smooth. Store in a sealable container.

SPICED DRIED APPLES Using a mandolin, thinly slice apples, revealing their cute cores. Toss apple slices with the maple syrup, lemon juice, and salt. Layer the apples on teflex sheets and sprinkle with apple pie spice. Dehydrate overnight at 115 degrees, flip, and continue to dehydrate for approximately 12 more hours until completely dry.

continued

Apple Pie ... continued

ROSEMARY OLIVE OIL CRUST AND CRUMBLE Mix all the dry ingredients together, and in small batches, powder everything into a fine flour using a high-speed blender. Chop the rosemary leaves and blend with the rest of the wet ingredients until well broken down. Add the wet ingredients to the dry and mix well with hands. Crumble enough crust mixture to cover 1 teflex sheet. Dehydrate at 115 degrees for 8 hours or until dry.

With the remaining crust, press 2 1/2 tablespoons of mixture into 12 (3 1/2-inch) ring molds and dehydrate on a teflex sheet at 115 degrees overnight. Flip and continue to keep warm in the dehydrator.

ASSEMBLY We build these little apple pies individually. Remove the crusts from the dehydrator while still on the teflex sheet. Keeping the crusts and ring molds together, remove the crusts and place on a flat surface.

Toss a mixture of 1/2 cup Baked Apples and 2 tablespoons Apple Gel together in a small bowl for the first pie. Fill 1 ring mold with this mixture using a slotted spoon. Use the Apple Gel remaining in the bowl to make the next pie. Repeat this process for the number of pies you need to serve. Top each pie with some rosemary crumble.

For each serving, swirl some Cranberry Splash around the plate in a loose spiral motion. Using a wide offset spatula, place a ring mold of pie on the plate slightly off center. Carefully remove the ring molds.

Randomly place 3 Rosemary Milk Sorbet disks, 3 Cream Cheese Sorbet disks, and 3 Spiced Dried Apples in the Cranberry Splash per plate. Serve.

Flax gel is made by soaking 1 part flax seeds in 2 parts water overnight. Strain through a nut milk bag. The liquid is the flax gel. Save the seeds for other uses.

Lime Cheesecake.
GINGER CRUMBLE. LIME GEL.
COLA FOAM.

This dessert is probably our most unique offering. Lime and cola is actually somewhat of a traditional combination—remember Diet Coke with Lime? The flavor works so well together. Think of this as a coke float with a twist! —*MB*

LIME CHEESECAKE
2 cups cashews, soaked overnight
$1/2$ cup filtered water
$1/4$ cup agave nectar
1 teaspoon nutritional yeast
$1/4$ teaspoon sea salt
$1/4$ cup lime juice
$1/4$ cup lemon juice
$1/2$ cup coconut oil

GINGER CRUMBLE
2 cups cashew flour
1 cup almond flour
$3/4$ cup maple syrup
1 tablespoon freshly grated ginger
1 tablespoon vanilla extract
1 tablespoon cinnamon
1 teaspoon sea salt
6 tablespoons water

COLA FOAM
12 drops lime essential oil
$1/4$ teaspoon nutmeg
$1/2$ teaspoon vanilla extract
2 tablespoons agave nectar
$1/2$ teaspoon grapeseed oil
$1/2$ teaspoon lecithin
$1/2$ cup filtered water
$1/2$ teaspoon lemon juice
Pinch of cinnamon

LIME GEL
$1/2$ cup agave nectar
$1/4$ cup spinach juice*
10 drops lime essential oil
$2 1/2$ teaspoons lemon juice
$1/4$ cup cashews, soaked overnight
$1/2$ teaspoon lecithin
Pinch of xanthan gum

CITRUS GLASS
1 lime
1 orange
1 grapefruit
2 tablespoons maple syrup

LIME CHEESECAKE Using a high-speed blender, mix all ingredients except for coconut oil until completely smooth. Gradually pour in the oil with the blender running on a slow speed until combined. Pour into a small sheet pan with 2-inch high sides and freeze.

After frozen, cut into 12 even triangles and store in freezer. Remove from freezer and let temper before serving. Do not serve frozen.

GINGER CRUMBLE Mix all ingredients together until well combined. Evenly spread on a dehydrator tray and dehydrate at 115 degrees for 18–24 hours until completely dry.

continued

Lime Cheesecake ... continued

COLA FOAM Mix all ingredients in a high-speed blender. Store in a sealable container. When ready to serve, create foam by using an immersion blender.

LIME GEL Blend all ingredients in a high speed blender until incorporated and completely smooth. Strain, if needed.

CITRUS GLASS Slice the citrus fruit very thin using a mandolin. Brush with maple syrup. Dehydrate on mesh sheets at 115 degrees overnight or until completely dry and crisp.

ASSEMBLY Using a squeeze bottle, dot each chilled serving plate with about a tablespoon of Lime Gel.

Spoon 3 tablespoons of Ginger Crumbs in 3 piles on each plate. Place a cheesecake triangle on top of each crumb pile. Spoon Cola Foam on top of each triangle. Top each cheesecake with Citrus Glass, using one of each citrus.

Using an electric juicer, juice 1 cup spinach for approximately $1/4$ cup juice.

Passion Fruit.
MELON. BERRIES. WHITE CHOCOLATE.

Passion fruit purée can be found in some specialty markets or online. The combination with melon is sweet, exotic, and tropical. —*MB*

PASSION FRUIT MOUSSE
1 cup passion fruit purée
$2/3$ cup flax gel (page 138)
$1/2$ teaspoon xanthan gum
$3/4$ cup agave nectar
$1/4$ cup water
$1/2$ vanilla bean, scraped

MELON SORBET
2 cups chopped honeydew
  melon
1 tablespoon honey

1 tablespoon agave nectar
1 teaspoon lime juice

BERRIES
2 cups fresh berries, of choice

WHITE CHOCOLATE
$1/4$ cup cacao butter, melted
1 tablespoon macadamia butter
1 teaspoon lecithin
$1/2$ teaspoon vanilla extract
$1/4$ cup maple powder

$1/4$ cup cashews, soaked
  overnight

LEMON BALM HONEY
2 cups packed lemon balm
  leaves
1 cup orange blossom honey
2 tablespoons warm water
Pinch of sea salt

GARNISH
Edible flowers

PASSION FRUIT MOUSSE Blend all ingredients in a high-speed blender. Freeze in Pacojet containers using a Pacojet machine following manufacturer's instructions or use a standard ice cream machine.

MELON SORBET Blend melon in a high-speed blender and strain through a chinois strainer. This removes excess pulp and produces a smoother texture. Add remaining ingredients to a high-speed blender and blend until combined. Freeze using your favorite ice cream machine.

WHITE CHOCOLATE Using a high-speed blender, blend cacao butter, macadamia butter, and lecithin until smooth. Add vanilla and maple powder to blender and blend until smooth. Add cashews and blend again until completely smooth and liquefied. Pour mixture into a squeeze bottle. Put a teflex sheet on a flat tray and, using the squeeze bottle, draw designs with the mixture. Freeze. Once set, store pieces layered between parchment paper in a flat sealable container in the freezer.

LEMON BALM HONEY Using a high-speed blender, blend all ingredients. Strain.

ASSEMBLY Scoop 2 heaping tablespoons of Passion Fruit Mousse into a 4-inch ring mold placed in the middle of wide, flat bowl for each serving. Spread mousse evenly in the bottom of the mold. Using a small ice cream scoop, put 5 scoops of Melon Sorbet on top of mousse. Place berries around the scoops of sorbet and drizzle with Lemon Balm Honey using a squeeze bottle. Top with a few pieces of the frozen White Chocolate. Garnish with flowers.

BUILDING A JUICE OR A SMOOTHIE IS JUST LIKE BUILDING ANY OTHER RECIPE. It must have balance. Too often these healthy beverages are created without considering the flavor combination. Our product is different because we approach these recipes as chefs—thinking about ingredients that go together seasonally, functionally, and as a flavor profile. We dare to say that each of these recipes is incredibly unique—and might just get ingrained in your sensory memory. —*MB*

Sipped

NUT MILK

Nut milks are used in several of the recipes in this cookbook. This is our standard recipe for making a variety of tasty milks. —MB

1/2 cup almonds, pistachios, Brazil, or hazelnuts, soaked 4–6 hours	2 cups water Pinch of sea salt 1 tablespoon coconut butter, optional	1 tablespoon honey, 2 dates, or sweetener of choice, optional

Using a high-speed blender, blend all ingredients until smooth. Strain out pulp through a chinois strainer or nut milk bag.

Smoothies

BEET. COCONUT. LIME.

SERVES 1–2

The combination of beet and coconut is somewhat unexpected in a smoothie, but the flavor is remarkable. The subtle sweetness of the coconut combined with the sweet earthiness of the beet is exotic and delicious!

1 cup coconut meat 1 1/2 cups coconut water	1/2 cup beet juice* 1 tablespoon lime juice	Pinch of sea salt

Using a high-speed blender, blend all ingredients until smooth.

Using an electric juicer, juice 1 large beet for 1/2 cup juice.

OLIVE LEAF. KALE. AVOCADO. PEAR. MINT.

SERVES 1–2

Using avocado in a smoothie is a great way to get creaminess without the typical overpowering flavor of banana. Avocados are low in sugar and high in healthy fats so this smoothie is a bit more satisfying than your typical all fruit version. Olive leaf extract is one of my new favorite supplements—it has a tea-like flavor and is packed with antioxidants and cancer fighting properties. This smoothie makes a great lunch.

1/2 avocado
1 pear
2 cups coconut water
1/2 cup kale

2 tablespoons mint leaves
2 to 3 drops olive leaf extract
Pinch of salt

Using a high-speed blender, blend all ingredients until smooth.

FIG. ORANGE. PISTACHIO. NUTMEG.

SERVES 1–2

The recipe for this smoothie was conceived from Matthew's Mediterranean culinary roots with a Moroccan influence. If you can get fresh figs, they make this smoothie absolutely amazing. It is perfect for a late summer breakfast when figs are at their ripest.

2 to 3 fresh figs (or 2 to 3 dried)
2 cups pistachio milk (page 146)

2 to 3 tablespoons orange zest
1 teaspoon vanilla extract
Pinch of nutmeg
Pinch of sea salt

Using a high-speed blender, blend all ingredients until smooth.

BRAZIL NUT. BANANA. CARROT. TURMERIC.

Brazil nut milk is my favorite nut milk. I once met an older woman with incredible skin and she credited the Brazil nut. For some reason that story stuck. Either way it tastes delicious, and is full of trace minerals and healthy fats. Carrots are, of course, full of vitamin A (beta carotene), which makes them great for the skin. And turmeric is a super skin spice that reduces inflammation and can improve acne, psoriasis, eczema, and other blemishes. This smoothie is super skin food!

1 cup Brazil nut milk
  (page 146)
1/2 frozen banana
1 cup carrot juice

2 tablespoons fresh turmeric
  juice (or 1 teaspoon dried)
1 teaspoon vanilla extract,
  optional

Pinch of cayenne, optional
Pinch of sea salt

Using a high-speed blender, blend all ingredients until smooth.

CACAO. CHAGA. COCONUT. CINNAMON.

Chaga is an ingredient that is new to us on the superfood list, although it is not new at all. Sometimes called the "Mushroom of Immortality," it is actually a fungus that grows on the birch tree. It is more commonly found in northern climates—like Maine, where you can easily find fresh, local chaga. It is associated with a variety of health benefits. It is said to increase endurance, aid in longevity, ward off cancer, and increase immunity, and is full of other antioxident and mineral properties. With so many health claims, we feel that it is absolutely a great addition.

2 cups coconut milk
1/4 cup cacao nibs

1 teaspoon chaga mushroom
  powder
1 vanilla bean

Pinch of cinnamon
Pinch of sea salt

Using a high-speed blender, blend all ingredients until smooth.

Juices

MK'S GREEN JUICE

SERVES 1–2

This is Matthew's favorite juice—hence the name. The flavor is perfectly tart and sweet—full of vitamin C and digestive aids; it is a great juice to have first thing in the morning.

1/2 pineapple	2 to 3 leaves kale	1 lime
1 apple	1/2 bunch parsley	1 (1-inch) chunk ginger
1 fennel bulb	1 lemon	

Run all ingredients through juicer.

PEACH. FENNEL. LEMON. GINGER. OREGANO OIL.

SERVES 1–2

This juice is only worth making when fresh peaches are in season. The fresher the better! The sweet juice of peach balances out the other spicy flavors. If you can't find oregano oil, you can leave it out—but if you have a cold it is worth the kick!

2 peaches	1 (1-inch) chunk ginger
1 fennel bulb	1 to 2 drops oregano oil
1 lemon	

Run peaches, fennel, lemon, and ginger through juicer. Stir in oregano oil.

BEET. GRAPEFRUIT. TURMERIC. ROMAINE.

Beets are nature's super root. They are detoxifying, fortifying, and liver cleansing, and the list goes on. Unlike some other root vegetables, beets actually lose a lot of their nutrition in the cooking process. Beets are also high in antioxidants, nitrates, and anti-inflammatory properties. We like to combine it with turmeric to enhance all of those benefits. This drink is great for workout recovery!

1 medium beet
1 grapefruit
1 (1-inch) chunk turmeric

1/2 large head romaine lettuce
1 lemon
Pinch of sea salt

Run all ingredients through juicer.

WATERMELON. TOMATO. LIME. CAYENNE. SALT.

This juice was my staple all summer. The health benefits in this combination are endless. Packed with the antioxidant lycopene, it is a free radical fighter at the highest level. Watermelon and tomato are both intensely packed with nutrients, as well as being high in water content, so they really help balance the system and aid in weight loss. The flavor is like a cocktail and would make an excellent base for a tequila or vodka addition.

1/2 small watermelon
2 medium tomatoes
1 lime

Pinch of cayenne
Pinch of sea salt

Run all ingredients through juicer.

Tea and Brews

KOMBUCHA

We owe much of our development in beverage fermentation to our academy team. They have been laboriously involved in all of these processes and have contributed to the consistency of each recipe. Sean Murray, Cristina Arcila, Kaia Harper, and Megan Massoth have each made a contribution to these recipes. The art of fermentation is truly fascinating and beneficial. Enjoy!

The recorded history of kombucha began in Ukraine and Russia during the late nineteenth century, though most people believe it was Chinese. Stories claim kombucha, famously known as the "Godly Tsche (tee-chee) [i.e., tea]" during the Chinese Qin Dynasty (221–206 BCE), was "a beverage with magical powers enabling people to live forever."

Kombucha contains multiple species of yeast and bacteria, as well as the organic acids, active enzymes, amino acids, and polyphenols produced by those microbes. For the home brewer, there is no way to know the amounts of the components unless a sample is sent to a laboratory. The tea is fermented with the use of a mother, also referred to as a mushroom or a SCOBY (Symbiotic Colony of Bacteria and Yeast). The SCOBY is scientifically classified as a zoogleal mat (ZOE-uh-glee-al).

Final kombucha may contain some of the following components depending on the source of the culture: acetic acid, which provides much anti-microbial activity; butyric acid, gluconic acid, glucuronic acid, lactic acid, malic acid, oxalic acid, usnic acid, as well as some B vitamins.

Due to the acidic fermentation process used in its brewing, Kombucha contains ethyl alcohol in amounts that vary from 0.5 percent to 1.5 percent, depending on anaerobic brewing time and proportions of microbes. Commercial preparations are typically 0.5 percent for distribution and safety reasons.

POTENTIAL BENEFITS

- » Restores hair color
- » Thickens hair
- » Increases skin health
- » Dissolves gallstones
- » Increases energy
- » Lengthens lifespan
- » Speeds healing
- » Lowers cholesterol
- » Lowers blood pressure
- » Improves digestion
- » Increases blood circulation
- » Eliminates wrinkles/skin humectant
- » Improves menopausal symptoms
- » Strengthens leg muscles
- » Chickenpox /herpes zoster remedy
- » Colitis/improves digestion/nervous stomach
- » Poultice for wounds/ulcers
- » Cleanses gallbladder
- » Lessens anxiety and helps you adapt to stress
- » Levels glucose
- » Protects teeth from cavities
- » Activates glandular system

SUPPLIES AND INGREDIENTS

MAKES 1 QUART (MULTIPLY RECIPE FOR LARGER BATCHES)

2 to 3 tablespoons unflavored organic caffeinated tea (black, green, mate, pu-erh) 1/4 cup sugar 1 quart-size glass jar	A plastic or wooden spoon Room temperature water 1/2 cup brewed kombucha (from previous batch)	1 SCOBY A fine-weave kitchen towel Rubber band

Brew 1 cup of tea and combine with sugar in jar. Using a plastic or wooden spoon, stir to dissolve the sugar. Once sugar has completely dissolved into the tea, add room temperature water until the jar is halfway full. Check to make sure the mixture is not uncomfortably hot as this can harm the SCOBY.

When the mixture has reached an acceptable temperature, add previously brewed kombucha and more water until there is 1–2 inches of free space remaining at the top of the jar.

ALWAYS WASH HANDS BEFORE HANDLING SCOBY

If your SCOBY did not come in a starter fluid or liquid medium, use store bought kombucha or proceed without it. Add SCOBY and cover with kitchen towel, using the rubber band to secure. (This is to prevent fruit flies from getting to the SCOBY).

Allow SCOBY to ferment tea for approximately 1–2 weeks, tasting every 5 days. The finished kombucha should be slightly sweet, with a subtle acidic aftertaste.

Once tea is fermented, you should now have 2 SCOBY's, a mother (the original) and a baby (the new one), though they may have stuck together. You can use them both to start a new batch, pull them apart and use them to start 2 new batches of kombucha, or give 1 to a friend. They are also great for your compost.

SECONDARY FERMENTATION If you'd like to flavor your kombucha, and add a little fizz, portion fermented kombucha liquid into small bottles or jars, adding fruit juice at an approximately 3:1 ratio. Seal jar or bottle and allow the mixture to ferment for 2–3 more days. Chill, and enjoy. Be careful when opening your flavored kombucha, as carbonation has likely built up during the secondary fermentation.

NOTES *If you want to keep your SCOBY but aren't ready to start a new batch of kombucha, put the SCOBY in a glass jar with a tight-fiting lid and enough kombucha liquid to cover it. Store in the refrigerator.*

Experiment with different flavors and brew times, but the liquid to sweetener ratio needs to stay the same. Never use metal when making kombucha, only glass, wood, or plastic.

Kombucha can be brewed with herbal teas, but caffeine is required to retain the health of your SCOBY. A good rule is to make sure that a third of the tea used contains caffeine, or that the SCOBY is brewed with a caffeinated tea at least every third batch. Refrain from using teas that are heavily flavored with oils, as this could harm the colony of bacteria and yeast in your SCOBY.

Kefir

Kefir grains are found all over the world. They are colonies of probiotic yeast and bacteria that can be used to ferment liquids. Dairy kefir grains originated in Eastern Europe and Russia, and are used traditionally in those cultures. Water kefir grains originated in Mexico and are called tibicos. Kefir grains can be grown in water or coconut water, and the resulting liquid can be flavored with fruit or vegetable juices. Plain water kefir or coconut water kefir can also be used to ferment cheeses in place of the liquid in the recipe. To obtain water kefir grains, order online or acquire from a friend or local store.

Water kefir grains cannot be grown from scratch—they have to come from a donor. The good news is that you only need a very small amount to start growing them. Once they are growing and healthy, you can donate some of your new grains to others so they can grow their own.

We do use white sugar in kefir, as it is the best source of food for them. All of the sugar gets eaten in the fermentation process and none of it will remain at the end of the fermentation. Look for a high quality source of sugar (vegan, organic, etc.), as conventional varieties of sugar tend to be highly GMO.

GROWING WATER KEFIR

2 to 3 tablespoons water kefir grains	1 quart pure water 1/4 cup white sugar	2 teaspoons molasses, optional

Place all ingredients in a glass jar and seal. Allow to stand at room temperature for up to 48 hours. Strain the liquid and reserve the grains. The resulting water can be consumed as is or added to smoothies for an extra boost of probiotics.

You should notice a small increase in the volume of the kefir grains. Repeat this process until you have enough grains to keep this process going and also make coconut kefir.

When you team up the previous process of growing the grains with the next instructions on how to make the actual kefir, you should be able to provide your daily kefir requirements on an ongoing basis.

COCONUT KEFIR

1/4 cup water kefir grains
1 quart young coconut water

Combine the kefir grains and the coconut water in a jar. Allow to stand for up to 48 hours at room temperature. You can check every 12 hours to make sure the fermentation isn't going too far.

You'll know if it's strong enough by taste testing. After you've made a few batches you'll get a feel of how you prefer it. The general rule is that the more grains you have in the water, the less time it will need to develop.

Strain the coconut kefir from the kefir grains and reserve the grains for another batch or to grow more. Set the coconut water kefir aside for a second stage fermentation. You can store the grains in a sealed container in the refrigerator in a small amount of kefir liquid.

Young coconut water doesn't have enough sugar to actually make the kefir grains grow, but it does have enough sugar to make the coconut water ferment into kefir.

TO FLAVOR

1/2 to 1 cup juice of choice

Combine the coconut kefir and juice in a jar. Leave to stand at room temperature for 48 hours. This will cause a second stage fermentation where the kefir will break down the sugars in the juice and go fizzy.

Modernist Equipment and Ingredients

EQUIPMENT

Having proper equipment is the key to having a functional kitchen. Whether you are preparing food for at-home enjoyment or preparing food for a professional environment, having the right tools makes the experience much more efficient and enjoyable. Some of the tools we have used in the making of this book certainly fall into the luxury category; these are not necessarily items most people have access to. Do not be discouraged. The beauty of this book is that most of these recipes can be prepared with or without these specialty items. Our goal is to introduce you to modernist techniques in order to provide an education on these tools and how they are used.

A well-stocked kitchen requires little more than high quality products, organized mise en place, and a sharp knife. A high-speed blender and juicer fall second in line to making your kitchen work for you. Most of these other items can be invested in over time. Please use this chapter as reference.

ANTI-GRIDDLE
The Anti-Griddle is produced by PolyScience. It is an advanced piece of food science technology. It works as a reverse heated griddle, and removes heat instantly. The result is flash freezing and enables you to quickly turn sauces, liquids, gels, creams, and other foods into a cool, crunchy texture.
http://cuisinetechnology.com/

BLENDERS
We use the Vitamix and Blendtec blenders interchangeably. Both are high-quality, high-powered blenders that are ideal in advanced food preparation.
https://www.vitamix.com/
http://www.blendtec.com/

DEHYDRATORS
Dehydrators are used to remove moisture from a dish to either reduce a liquid and make a thick sauce, or to remove all liquid completely to create a crisp texture. The Sedona Dehydrator is what we choose to use.
http://www.tribest.com/

ISI SIPHON
Isi is the industry leader in siphon chargers. This tool is a canister that injects CO_2 into liquids to create sodas, whipped creams, and other aerated products.
http://www.isi.com/us/culinary

JUICERS
While there are many juicer brands available, the Breville juicer is our favorite. It is a centrifugal juicer that is fast, versatile, functional, and easy to clean.
http://www.breville.com/

MANDOLIN
A mandolin is a tool used for slicing in uniform cuts. With various attachments, you have the ability to julienne and slice fruits and vegetables into paper-thin pieces.
http://www.williams-sonoma.com/

MICROPLANE

A microplane is a razor sharp, ultra-fine grating tool most commonly used to grate citrus zest and spices.

http://www.williams-sonoma.com/

MINIPACK VACUUM MACHINE

The minipack is used to vacuum-seal food in preparation for the sous vide, marinating, and cook-chill.

http://www.minipack.us/

PACOJET

The Pacojet is an advanced form of emulsion. This piece of equipment is used to process food in calibrated portions, resulting in creams, sauces, mousses, and ice creams that have the texture of being freshly made.

http://www.pacojet.com/

SMOKING GUN

The smoking gun is a hand-held alternative smoking method that allows you to impart rich, concentrated, smoky flavor without all of the mess and hassle of a traditional smoker. Portions can be much smaller and precise, and can be used on virtually any food.

http://cuisinetechnology.com/

SOUS VIDE BY POLYSCIENCE

Sous vide is a technique of preparing food by vacuum sealing and cooking in a circulating water bath at low temperatures. Sous vide preparation produces foods that are tender and evenly cooked.

http://cuisinetechnology.com/

INGREDIENTS

This is a list of ingredients that fall into the category of molecular gastronomy or molecular cuisine. These ingredients are not commonly found in most kitchens, but are easy to find and to use. They help produce the techniques that are associated with molecular cuisine such as foams, powders, gels, and spherification. Although the names are somewhat obscure, they are all natural, plant-based derivatives. All ingredients are available at Whole Foods or other health food stores.

AGAR

Agar is a seaweed-based gelling agent that is often used in Asian desserts. It serves as a vegetarian gelatin substitute. It is usually found in powder or flake form.

IRISH MOSS

Irish moss, or carrageenan, is a species of red algae seaweed that is used for culinary purposes as a thickener and stabilizer.

LECITHIN

Lecithin is a brownish-yellow fatty substance that is extracted from either plant or animal protein. An egg yolk is one of the most common sources of lecithin. Lecithin is used in recipes to emulsify ingredients and create a smooth, creamy texture.

TAPIOCA MALTODEXTRIN

Tapioca maltodextrin is a starch derived from the cassava root. Most starches, like flour, take in and can thicken water and sauces. Maltodextrin does the opposite. When added to a fat, it absorbs all the liquid and creates a powder.

www.willpowder.com

XANTHAN GUM

Xanthan Gum is made by fermenting corn sugar with the xanthomonas campestris bacteria. Xanthum is used as an emulsifier, thickener, and stabilizer. It is commonly used in gluten-free baking.

Index

METRIC CONVERSION CHART

VOLUME MEASUREMENTS		WEIGHT MEASUREMENTS		TEMPERATURE CONVERSION	
U.S.	METRIC	U.S.	METRIC	FAHRENHEIT	CELSIUS
1 teaspoon	5 ml	1/2 ounce	15 g	250	120
1 tablespoon	15 ml	1 ounce	30 g	300	150
1/4 cup	60 ml	3 ounces	90 g	325	160
1/3 cup	75 ml	4 ounces	115 g	350	180
1/2 cup	125 ml	8 ounces	225 g	375	190
2/3 cup	150 ml	12 ounces	350 g	400	200
3/4 cup	175 ml	1 pound	450 g	425	220
1 cup	250 ml	2 1/4 pounds	1 kg	450	230